COLLECTED WORKS OF RENÉ GUÉNON

TRADITIONAL FORMS AND COSMIC CYCLES

RENÉ GUÉNON

TRADITIONAL FORMS
AND COSMIC CYCLES

Translator
Henry D. Fohr

Editor
Samuel D. Fohr

SOPHIA PERENNIS

HILLSDALE NY

Originally published in French as
Formes Traditionnelles et Cycles Cosmiques
© Éditions Gallimard 1970
English translation © Sophia Perennis 2001
First English Edition 2003
Second Impression 2004

Series editor: James R. Wetmore

For information, address:
Sophia Perennis, P.O. Box 611
Hillsdale NY 12529
sophiaperennis.com

Library of Congress Cataloging-in-Publication Data

Guénon, René
[Formes Traditionnelles et cycles cosmiques. English]
Traditional forms and cosmic cycles / René Guénon ; translated by
Henry D. Fohr ; edited by Samuel D. Fohr

p. cm.
Includes bibliographical references and index.
ISBN 0 900588 16 0 (pbk: alk. paper)
ISBN 0 900588 17 9 (cloth: alk. paper)
1. Time—Religious aspects I. Title
BL65.T5 B65 2001
291.2'4—dc21   2001000430

THE PUBLISHER
GIVES SPECIAL THANKS TO
HENRY D. AND JENNIE L. FOHR
FOR MAKING THIS EDITION POSSIBLE

CONTENTS

EDITORIAL NOTE

THE PAST CENTURY HAS WITNESSED an erosion of earlier cultural values as well as a blurring of the distinctive characteristics of the world's traditional civilizations, giving rise to philosophic and moral relativism, multiculturalism, and dangerous fundamentalist reactions. As early as the 1920s, the French metaphysician René Guénon (1886–1951) had diagnosed these tendencies and presented what he believed to be the only possible reconciliation of the legitimate, although apparently conflicting, demands of outward religious forms, 'exoterisms', with their essential core, 'esoterism'. His works are characterized by a foundational critique of the modern world coupled with a call for intellectual reform; a renewed examination of metaphysics, the traditional sciences, and symbolism, with special reference to the ultimate unanimity of all spiritual traditions; and finally, a call to the work of spiritual realization. Despite their wide influence, translation of Guénon's works into English has so far been piecemeal. The *Sophia Perennis* edition is intended to fill the urgent need to present them in a more authoritative and systematic form. A complete list of Guénon's works, given in the order of their original publication in French, follows this note.

Traditional Forms and Cosmic Cycles is a wide-ranging collection of articles that delve into traces of ancient, indeed protohistoric, traditions. Although they must remain fragments, as Guénon did not return to many of these themes, it would have been regrettable to leave such fascinating articles buried in old journals, and so this posthumous collection is now offered to Anglophone readers for the first time. The book opens with the key article 'The Doctrine of Cosmic Cycles', followed by two pieces on Atlantis and Hyperborea. Two sections follow, concerned respectively with the Hebrew Tradition and the Egyptian Tradition. The former comprises five articles concerned primarily with the Kabbalah and the Science of Numbers, and the latter includes three articles on Hermes and the Hermetic Tradition. Book reviews are inserted at relevant points

The sources of the original French articles collected in this book are as follows: pt. I, chap. 1, *Études Traditionnelles*, October 1938 (first appeared in English in the *Journal of the Indian Society of Oriental Art*, June–December 1937, dedicated to A.K. Coomaraswamy on the occasion of his sixtieth birthday; pt. II, chap. 2, *Voile d'Isis*, October 1929 (the three reviews appeared, respectively, in *Études Traditionnelles*, December 1949, October 1937, and January 1949); pt. II, chap. 2, *Voile d'Isis*, August–September 1931; pt. III, chap. 1, *Voile d'Isis*, December 1931; pt. III, chap. 2, *Voile d'Isis*, May 1933; pt. III, chap. 3, *Voile d'Isis*, August–September 1933; pt. III, chap. 4, *Ignis*, 1925; pt. III, chap. 5, *Voile d'Isis*, December 1930 (the two reviews appeared, respectively, in *Études Traditionnelles*, July 1936 and December 1936); pt. IV, chap. 1, *Voile d'Isis* April 1931; pt. IV, chap. 2, *Voile d'Isis*, April 1932; pt. IV, chap. 3, *Études Traditionnelles*, December 1936 (the eight reviews appeared, respectively, in *Études Traditionnelles*, November 1936, November 1937, June 1938, January 1945, January 1945, January–February 1948, January 1945, and December 1949).

Guénon often uses words or expressions set off in 'scare quotes'. To avoid clutter, single quotation marks have been used throughout. As for transliterations, Guénon was more concerned with phonetic fidelity than academic usage. The system adopted here reflects the views of scholars familiar both with the languages and Guénon's writings. Brackets indicate editorial insertions, or, within citations, Guénon's additions. Wherever possible, references have been updated, and English editions substituted.

The present translation is based on the work of Henry Fohr, edited by his son Samuel Fohr. The entire text was checked for accuracy and further revised by Patrick Moore. For help with selected chapters thanks go to Cecil Bethell, John Champoux, and John Ahmed Herlihy. A special debt of thanks is owed to Cecil Bethell, who typed, then revised and proofread the text at several stages, and provided the index. Cover design by Michael Buchino and Gray Henry, based on a drawing by Guénon's friend and collaborator Ananda K. Coomaraswamy.

THE WORKS
OF RENÉ GUÉNON

FOREWORD

THE ARTICLES COLLECTED in this volume represent perhaps the
most 'original' aspect of René Guénon's work, and perhaps also the
most disconcerting. It could have been entitled *Fragments of an
Unknown History*, but a history that includes protohistory and prehistory, since it takes its start with the primordial tradition contemporaneous with the beginnings of present humanity.

The articles are fragments, and could only be such, for Guénon
himself doubtless could not have presented this history as an uninterrupted narrative since he drew its elements from so many different traditional sources. And they are fragments also in the sense
that we have brought together here texts not yet incorporated in
previous volumes, either by Guénon himself or by the compilers of
the collections of his articles so far published after his death.

Such as they are, these articles seemed to us to open so many new
vistas to the Western reader of today that it would have been regrettable to leave them buried in journal collections accessible only in a
few large public libraries. We alluded to his many traditional
sources, and this is the place to recall that Guénon once wrote that
his sources did not carry 'references'. This is even more true of the
texts brought together here than for other parts of Guénon's work.
Thus to our mind the present collection is intended mainly for
readers already acquainted to some extent with this work: the metaphysics Guénon has expounded will stand for them as surety for
this history of the Tradition.

Of the following texts it is perhaps those concerned with Hyperborea and Atlantis that will be the stumbling-block for many, for
almost everything said regarding them stands opposed to prevailing
scientific ideas in the West. Points of agreement might be more
numerous with the results of scientific research in the Soviet world,
but the latter are too imperfectly known to us as yet to be of any real
utility here.

Besides, given the prehistoric character of the epochs to which the Hyperborean and Atlantean traditions carry us back, we could only evoke some indications, at best some groups of them, for the most part drawn from ethnography, comparative linguistics, or comparative religion. Then again we could mention the similarity of certain rites, and the more or less close kinship of several others, particularly the rite of circumcision practised on both sides of the Atlantic. Architecture and archaeology would doubtless provide some support. We know that after denying it for generations, scientists have had to admit, since the discovery of some funerary crypts, that the pyramids of the New World were used not only as temples, but also as tombs—and sometimes as observatories—exactly like those of Egypt. But the fact remains, we repeat, that from the point of view of official science these provide only indications, not certainties, as to the presence of man on an Atlantean continent, the existence itself of this last, in previous geologic epochs, no longer being debated.

Since it serves only as a preamble, the study on cosmic cycles with which the collection opens does not offer any particular difficulties, the existence of a doctrine of cycles in Hindu tradition being generally known in the West. We know now that cyclical theories also exist in Jewish Kabbalah and in Islamic esoterism.

To give more coherence to the collection, we have kept, besides the studies on Hyperborea and Atlantis, only those that concern non-Christian traditions that have had a direct influence on the Western world, that is, the Hebrew tradition and the Egyptian and Greco-Latin traditions. Celtism is not included, nor is Islam. This is not out of lack of respect for the role of these two traditions—far from it—but simply because those of Guénon's articles that deal with Celtism have been included in the collection called *Symbols of Sacred Science*, including 'The Holy Grail' (chap. 4), 'The Triple Precinct of the Druids' (chap. 10), 'The Land of the Sun' (chap. 12), and 'The Wild Boar and the Bear' (chap. 24). As for Islam, the only article having any connection with the present subject, entitled 'The Mysteries of the Letter *Nūn*', is found in the same book (chap. 23).

As for the Hebraic and Egyptian traditions, the studies contained in the present collection are complemented by 'Cain and Abel' in

The Reign of Quantity and the Signs of the Times (chap. 21) and by 'Seth' in *Symbols of Sacred Science* (chap. 20).

Having said all this, it should be added that the present volume cannot in any case be entirely separated from the following three books now considered in their totality: *The King of the World, The Reign of Quantity and the Signs of the Times,* and *Symbols of Sacred Science.* And one may perhaps be permitted to add that the traditional cosmological knowledge to be found in these four works constitutes a sum-total of such knowledge that has no equivalent in any language.

ROGER MARIDORT

PART I

1

SOME REMARKS
ON THE DOCTRINE
OF COSMIC CYCLES

WE HAVE OFTEN BEEN ASKED, regarding allusions we have been
led to make here and there to the Hindu doctrine of cosmic cycles
and its equivalents in other traditions, whether we might give, if not
a complete explanation, at least an overview sufficient to reveal its
broad outlines. In truth, this seems an almost impossible task, not
only because the question is very complex in itself, but especially
owing to the extreme difficulty of expressing these things in a European language and in a way that is intelligible to the present-day
Western mentality, which has had no practice whatsoever with this
kind of thinking. All that is really possible, in our opinion, is to try
to clarify a few points with remarks such as those that follow, which
can only raise suggestions about the meaning of the doctrine in
question rather than to really explain it.

In the most general sense of the term, a cycle must be considered
as representing the process of development of some state of manifestation, or, in the case of minor cycles, of one of the more or less
restricted and specialized modalities of that state. Moreover, in virtue of the law of correspondence which links all things in universal
Existence, there is necessarily and always a certain analogy, either
among different cycles of the same order or among the principal
cycles and their secondary divisions. This is what allows us to use
one and the same mode of expression when speaking about them,
although this must often be understood only symbolically, for the
very essence of all symbolism is precisely founded on the analogies

and correspondences which really exist in the nature of things. We allude here especially to the 'chronological' form under which the doctrine of cycles is presented: since a *Kalpa* represents the total development of a world, that is to say of a state or degree of universal Existence, it is obvious that one cannot speak literally about its duration, computed according to some temporal measure, unless this duration relates to a state of which time is one of the determining conditions, as in our world. Everywhere else, this duration and the succession that it implies can have only a purely symbolic value and must be transposed analogically, for temporal succession is then only an image, both logical and ontological, of an 'extra-temporal' series of causes and effects. On the other hand, since human language cannot directly express any condition other than those of our own state, such a symbolism is by that very fact sufficiently justified and must be regarded as perfectly natural and normal.

We do not intend to deal just now with the most extensive cycles, such as the *Kalpas*; we will limit ourselves to those which develop within our *Kalpa*, that is, the *Manvantaras* and their subdivisions. At this level, the cycles have a character that is at once cosmic and historical, for they particularly concern terrestrial humanity, while at the same time being closely linked to events occurring in our world but outside of the history of humanity. There is nothing to surprise us here, for the idea of seeing human history as somehow isolated from all the rest is exclusively modern and sharply opposed to what is taught by all traditions, which on the contrary unanimously affirm a necessary and constant correlation between the cosmic and the human orders.

The *Manvantaras*, or eras of successive *Manus*, are fourteen in number, forming two septenary series of which the first includes both past *Manvantaras* and our present one, and the second future *Manvantaras*. These two series, of which one relates to the past as well as to the present that is its immediate result, and the other to the future, can be linked with those of the seven *Svargas* and the seven *Pātālas*, which, from the point of view of the hierarchy of the degrees of existence or of universal manifestation, represent the states respectively higher and lower than the human state, or anterior and posterior with respect to that state if one places oneself at the viewpoint of the causal connection of the cycles symbolically described, as always, under the analogy of a temporal succession. This last point of view is obviously the most important here, for it enables us to see within our *Kalpa* a kind of reduced image of the totality of the cycles of universal manifestation according to the analogical relation we mentioned earlier; and in this sense one could say that the succession of *Manvantaras* in a way marks a reflection of other worlds in ours. To confirm this relationship, one could also note that the words *Manu* and *Loka* are both used as symbolic designations for the number 14; to say that this is simply a 'coincidence' would be to give proof of a complete ignorance of the profound reasons inherent in all traditional symbolism.

Yet another correspondence with the *Manvantaras* concerns the seven *Dvīpas* or 'regions' into which our world is divided. Although according to the proper meaning of the word that designates them these are represented as islands or continents distributed in a certain way in space, one must be careful not to take this literally and to regard them simply as different parts of present-day earth; in fact, they 'emerge' in turns and not simultaneously, which is to say that only one of them is manifested in the sensible domain over the course of a certain period. If that period is a *Manvantara*, one will have to conclude that each *Dvīpa* will have to appear twice in the *Kalpa* or once in each of the just mentioned septenary series; and from the relationship of these two series, which correspond to one another inversely as do all similar cases, particularly the *Svargas* and the *Pātālas*, one can deduce that the order of appearance for the *Dvīpas* will likewise have to be, in the second series, the inverse of what it was in the first. In sum, this is a matter of different 'states' of the terrestrial world rather than 'regions' properly speaking; the *Jambu-Dvīpa* really represents the entire earth in its present state, and if it is said to extend to the south of *Meru*, the 'axial' mountain around which our world revolves, this is because *Meru* is identified symbolically with the North Pole, so that the whole earth is really situated to the south with respect to it. To explain this more completely it would be necessary to develop the symbolism of the directions of space according to which the *Dvīpas* are distributed, as well as correspondences existing between this spatial symbolism and the temporal symbolism on which the whole doctrine of cycles rests; but since we cannot here go into these considerations, which alone would require a whole volume, we must be content with these summary indications, which can be easily completed by all who already have some knowledge of what is involved.

This way of envisaging the *Dvīpas* is also confirmed by concordant data from other traditions which also speak of 'seven lands', particularly Islamic esoterism and the Hebrew Kabbalah. Thus in the latter, even while these 'seven lands' are outwardly represented by as many divisions of the land of Canaan, they are related to the reigns of the 'seven kings of Edom' which clearly correspond to the seven *Manus* of the first series; and all are included in the 'Land of the Living' which represents the complete development of our world considered as realized permanently in its principial state. We can note here the coexistence of two points of view, one of succession, which refers to manifestation in itself, and the other of simultaneity, which refers to its principle or to what one could call its 'archetype'; and at root the correspondence between these two points of view is in a certain way equivalent to that between temporal symbolism and spatial symbolism, to which we just alluded in connection with the *Dvīpas* of the Hindu tradition.

In Islamic esoterism, the 'seven lands' appear, perhaps even more explicitly, as so many *tabaqāt* or 'categories' of terrestrial existence, which coexist and in a way interpenetrate, but only one of which is presently accessible to the senses while the others are in a latent state and can only be perceived exceptionally and under certain special conditions; these too are manifested outwardly in turn, during the different periods that succeed one another in the course of the total duration of this world. On the other hand, each of the 'seven lands' is governed by a *Quṭb* or 'Pole', which thus corresponds very clearly to the *Manu* of the period during which his land is manifested; and these seven *Aqṭāb* are subordinate to the supreme 'Pole' just as the different *Manus* are subordinate to the *Adi-Manu* or primordial *Manu*; but because these 'seven lands' coexist, they also in a certain respect exercise their functions in a permanent and simultaneous way. It is hardly necessary to point out that the designation of 'Pole' is closely related to the 'polar' symbolism of *Meru* which we just mentioned, for *Meru* itself has in any case its exact equivalent in the mountain of *Qāf* in Islamic tradition. Let us also add that the seven terrestrial 'Poles' are considered to be reflections of the seven celestial 'Poles' which preside respectively over the seven planetary heavens; and this naturally evokes the correspondence with the *Svargas* in Hindu doctrine, which shows in sum the perfect concordance in this regard between the two traditions.

We shall now consider the divisions of a *Manvantara*, that is to say the *Yugas*, which are four in number. First of all, and without dwelling on it at length, let us point out that this quaternary division of a cycle is susceptible of multiple applications and that it is in fact found in many cycles of a more particular order. One can cite as examples the four seasons of the year, the four weeks of the lunar month, and the four ages of human life; here too there is correspondence with a spatial symbolism, in this case principally related to the four cardinal points. On the other hand, we have often called attention to the obvious equivalence of the four *Yugas* with the four ages of gold, silver, bronze, and iron as they were known to Greco-Latin antiquity, in both cases, each period is marked by a degeneration in regard to the age that preceded it; and this, which is directly opposed to the idea of 'progress' as understood by the modern world, is very simply explained by the fact that every cyclical development, that is in sum every process of manifestation, quite truly constitutes a 'descent' since it necessarily implies a gradual distancing from the principle, and this is moreover the real meaning of the 'fall' in the Judeo-Christian tradition.

From one *Yuga* to the next the degeneration is accompanied by a decrease in duration, and this is thought to influence the length of human life; and what is most important in this respect are the ratios that exist between the respective durations of these different periods. If the total duration of the *Manvantara* is represented by 10, that of the *Krita-Yuga* or *Satya-Yuga* is 4, that of the *Treta-Yuga* is 3, that of the *Dvapara-Yuga* is 2, and that of the *Kali-Yuga* is 1. These numbers are also those belonging to the feet of the symbolic bull of *Dharma* which are represented as resting on the earth during the same periods. The division of the *Manvantara* is therefore carried out according to the formula $10 = 4 + 3 + 2 + 1$, which is, in reverse, that of the Pythagorean *Tetraktys*: $1 + 2 + 3 + 4 = 10$. This last formula corresponds to what the language of Western Hermeticism calls the 'circling of the square', and the other to the opposite problem of the 'squaring of the circle', which expresses precisely the relation of the end of a cycle to its beginning, that is, the integration of its total development. Here there is an entire symbolism both arithmetic and geometric which we can only indicate in passing so as not to digress too far from our principal subject.

As for the numbers given in different texts for the duration of the *Manvantara* and consequently for that of the *Yugas*, it must be understood that they are not to be regarded as a 'chronology' in the ordinary sense of the word, we mean as expressing a literal number of years; and this is also why certain apparent differences in these numbers do not really imply any contradiction. Generally speaking, it is only the number 4,320 that is to be considered in these figures, for a reason that we shall explain later, and not the many zeros that follow it, which may well be meant to lead astray those who wish to devote themselves to certain calculations. At first glance, such a precaution might seem strange, and yet it is easily explained: if the real duration of the *Manvantara* were known, and if in addition its starting-point were exactly determined, anyone could without difficulty draw therefrom deductions allowing him to foresee certain future events. But no orthodox tradition has ever encouraged inquiries by means of which someone might see more or less into the future, since in practice such a knowledge has more drawbacks than real advantages. This is why the starting-point and the duration of the *Manvantara* have always been more or less carefully concealed, either by adding or subtracting a given number of years from the real dates, or by multiplying or dividing the durations of the cyclical periods so as to conserve only their exact proportions; and we will add that certain correspondences have also sometimes been reversed for similar reasons.

If the duration of the *Manvantara* is 4,320, those of the four *Yugas* will respectively be 1,728, 1,296, 864, and 432; but by what number must we multiply them to obtain an expression of these durations in years? It is easy to see that all the cyclical numbers are directly related to the geometric division of the circle; thus $4,320 = 360 \times 12$.

Besides, there is nothing arbitrary or purely conventional in this division because, for reasons relating to the correspondence between arithmetic and geometry, it is normal for it to be carried out according to multiples of 3, 9, and 12, whereas decimal division is that best suited for the straight line. And yet this observation, although truly fundamental, would not enable us to go very far in determining cyclical periods if we did not also know that in the cosmic order their principal basis is the astronomical period of the precession of the equinoxes, of which the duration is 25,920 years, so that the displacement of the equinoctial points is one degree in 72 years. This number 72 is precisely a sub-multiple of 4,320 = 72 x 60, and 4,320 is in turn a sub-multiple of 25,920 = 4,320 x 6. The fact that we find in the precession of the equinoxes numbers linked to the division of the circle is yet another proof of its truly natural character; but the question that now arises is this: what multiple or sub-multiple of the astronomical period in question really corresponds to the duration of the *Manvantara*?

The period that appears most frequently in different traditions is in truth not so much the precession of equinoxes as its half; actually, it is this that corresponds in particular to the 'great year' of the Persians and the Greeks which is often expressed by approximation as either 12,000 or 13,000 years, its exact duration being 12,960 years. Given the very particular importance which is thus attributed to that period, it is to be presumed that the *Manvantara* will have to comprise a whole number of these 'great years'; but what will that number be? Here we find, elsewhere than in Hindu tradition, at least a precise indication which this time seems plausible enough to be accepted literally: among the Chaldeans, the duration of the reign of *Xisuthros*, which is manifestly identical to *Vaivasvata*, the *Manu* of the present era, is fixed at 64,800 years, or exactly five 'great years'. Let us note incidentally that the number 5, being that of the *bhūtas* or elements of the sensory world, must necessarily have a special importance from the cosmological point of view, something that tends to confirm the reality of such an evaluation; perhaps there is reason to consider a correlation between the five *bhūtas* and the successive five 'great years' in question, all the more so in fact since in the ancient traditions of Central America one encounters an explicit association of the elements with certain cyclical periods; but this question would require closer examination. However that may be, if such is indeed the real duration of the *Manvantara*, and if we continue to take as a base the number 4,320, which is equal to the third part of the 'great year', it is then by 15 that this number will have to be multiplied. On the other hand, the five 'great years' will naturally be distributed unequally but according to simple relationships among the four *Yugas*: the *Krita-Yuga* will contain 2 of them, the *Treta-Yuga* 1½, the *Dvapara-Yuga* 1, and the *Kali-Yuga* ½; these numbers are of course half of those we previously used when representing the duration of the *Manvantara* by 10. Expressed in ordinary years, these same durations of the four *Yugas* will be respectively 25,920, 19,440, 12,960, and 6,480 years, forming the total of 64,800 years; and it will be recognized that these numbers are at least within perfectly plausible limits and may very well correspond to the true chronology of present terrestrial humanity.

We will end these considerations here, for as concerns the starting-point of our *Manvantara* and consequently the exact point in its course where we are presently situated, we do not intend to risk an attempt to determine them. By all traditional data we know that we have been in the *Kali-Yuga* for a long time already; and we can say without fear of error that we are in an advanced phase, a phase whose description in the *Purānas* corresponds in the most striking fashion to the characteristics of our present epoch. But would it not be imprudent to wish to be more exact, and would this not inevitably end in the kinds of predictions to which traditional doctrine has, not without good reasons, posed so many obstacles?

REVIEWS

MIRCEA ELIADE: *Le Mythe de l'éternel retour: Archétypes et répétition* (Paris: Gallimard, 1961) [*The Myth of the Eternal Return* (Princeton: Princeton University Press, 1991)]. The title of this small volume, which does not exactly correspond to its contents, does not appear to us to be a very happy one, for it inevitably makes one think of the modern notions to which this term 'eternal return' is usually applied and which, besides confusing eternity with indefinite duration, imply the existence of a repetition that is impossible and clearly contrary to the true traditional notion of cycles, according to which there is only correspondence and not identity. In the final analysis there is in the case of the macrocosmic order a difference comparable to that which exists in the microcosmic order between the idea of reincarnation and that of the passage of the being through the multiple states of manifestation. But this is not in fact what Eliade's book is about, and what he means by 'repetition' is nothing other than the reproduction or rather the ritual imitation of 'what was in the beginning'. In an integrally traditional civilization, everything proceeds from 'celestial archetypes'; thus cities, temples, and dwellings are always erected according to a cosmic model; another related question, one which at root differs much less from the former than the author seems to think, is that of symbolic identification with the 'Center'. These are things about which we ourselves have often spoken;[1] Eliade has brought together numerous examples referring to the most diverse traditions which show quite well the universality and, we could say, the 'normality' of these ideas. He then goes on to the examination of rites properly so called, always from the same point of view; but there is one point on which we must state a serious reservation: he speaks of 'archetypes of profane activities', whereas precisely, as long as a civilization preserves an integrally traditional character, there are no profane activities. It seems to us that what he so designates is what has become profane as a result of a degeneration, which is something quite different, for then, and by that very fact, there can no longer be a question of 'archetypes', for the profane is such only because it is no longer linked to any transcendent principle. Besides, there is certainly nothing profane in the examples he gives (ritual dances, anointing of a king, traditional medicine). In what follows, the emphasis is more particularly on the question of the annual cycle and the rites linked to it. By virtue of the correspondence that exists between all cycles, the year itself may naturally be taken as a reduced image of the great cycles of universal manifestation, and this is what explains in particular that its beginning may be considered to have a 'cosmogonic' character. The idea of a 'regeneration of time', which the author interjects here, is not very clear, but it seems that what must be understood by

1. See especially *The King of the World.* ED.

this is the divine conservation of the manifested world, with which the ritual action is a true collaboration by virtue of the relations existing between the cosmic order and the human order. What is regrettable is that despite all of this he thinks he is obliged to speak of 'beliefs', whereas what is involved is the application of a very real knowledge and of traditional sciences which have a value altogether different from that of the profane sciences. And why must he also, in another concession to modern prejudices, excuse himself for having 'avoided all sociological or ethnographic interpretation', whereas on the contrary we could not praise the author too much for this abstention, especially when we recall to what extent other studies have been spoiled by such interpretations?

The last chapters are less interesting from our point of view, and they are in any case the most questionable, for what they contain is no longer a description of traditional ideas but rather Eliade's own reflections, from which he tries to draw a sort of 'philosophy of history'. Moreover, we do not see how cyclical conceptions would be opposed in any way to history (he even uses the expression 'refutation of history'), and in truth history cannot really have meaning except insofar as it expresses the unfolding of events within the course of the human cycle, although profane historians are no doubt scarcely capable of conceiving this. If the idea of 'misfortune' can in one sense be attached to 'historical existence', it is precisely because the course of the cycle is accomplished according to a descending movement. One must add that the final remarks on the 'terror of history' seem to us rather too much inspired by 'current events'.

GASTON GEORGEL: *Les Rythmes dans l'Histoire* (Belfort: Gaston Georgel, 1937). This book constitutes an essay on the application of cosmic cycles to the history of peoples and to the phases of growth and decadence in civilizations. It is truly a pity that in undertaking such a work the writer did not have at his disposal more complete traditional data, and that he knew some only through rather doubtful intermediaries who mingled with them their own imaginings. Nevertheless, he has seen that the essential thing to consider is the period of the precession of the equinoxes and its division, even though he adds some complications that seem of little use; but the terminology he adopts to designate certain secondary periods betrays a number of misunderstandings and confusions. Thus, the twelfth part of the precession certainly cannot be called a 'cosmic year'; that name would be much more fitting either for the entire period, or even more to its half, which is precisely the 'great year' of the ancients. On the other hand, the period of 25,765 years is probably borrowed from some hypothetical calculation of modern astronomers, but the duration traditionally indicated is 25,920 years. A singular consequence of this is that the author is sometimes led to take the exact numbers for certain divisions, for example 2,160 and 540, but then considers them as only 'approximate'. Let us add still one more observation on this subject: he thinks he has found a confirmation of the cycle of 539 years in certain biblical texts which suggest the number $77 \times 7 = 539$; but precisely here he should have taken $77 \times 7 + 1 = 540$, even if only by analogy with the jubilee year, which was not the 49th but really the 50th, or $7 \times 7 + 1 = 50$. As for applications, if there are correspondences and relationships that are not only curious but really worthy of note, we must say there are others which are much less striking or which even seem somewhat forced, to the point of recalling unfortunately the childishness of certain occultists. There would also be quite a few reservations to be made on other points, for example the fanciful figures set forth for the chronology of ancient civilizations. On the other hand, it would have been interesting to see whether the writer could have continued to get results of the same kind by expanding his field of inquiries, for there have been and still are many other peoples than those he considers. In any case, we do not think it possible to establish a general 'synchronism' because, for different peoples, the starting-point must likewise be different; and moreover, different civilizations do not simply succeed one another, they also coexist, as one can still witness today. In conclusion, the author has thought it well to indulge in several attempts at 'foreseeing the future', within rather restricted limits; that is one of the dangers of this kind of research, especially in our time, where so-called 'prophecies' are in such vogue. Certainly, no tradition has ever encouraged such things and it is even in order to obstruct them as much as possible rather than for any other reason that certain aspects of the doctrine of cycles have always been shrouded in obscurity.

GASTON GEORGEL: *Les Rythmes dans l'Histoire*. (Besançon: Éditions 'Servir', 1947). We reviewed this book when the first edition appeared (October 1937 issue); at the time, the author, as he indicates in the foreword of this new edition, knew almost nothing of the traditional data concerning cycles, to the point that it was only by good fortune that, starting from a strictly empirical viewpoint, he happened to suspect the importance of the precession of the equinoxes. The few remarks we made then had the consequence of turning him toward more detailed studies, for which we can certainly only congratulate ourselves, and we must express our thanks to him for what he is willing to say on our behalf. He has therefore modified and completed his work on many points, adding new chapters or paragraphs, one a history of the question of cycles, correcting various inaccuracies, and suppressing the doubtful considerations that he at first accepted on faith from occultist writers because he was able to compare them with more authentic data. We regret only that he forgot to replace the numbers 539 and 1,078 years with the correct numbers 540 and 1,080, something which the foreword however seemed to announce, all the more so because he did indeed rectify 2,156 years with 2,160, which introduces a certain apparent disagreement between the chapters dealing with these different cycles that are multiples of one another. It is also somewhat unfortunate that he retained the expressions 'cosmic year' and 'cosmic season' to designate periods much too short to really apply correctly (2,160 and of 540 years), which are rather, so to speak, only 'months' and 'weeks', all the more so since the name 'month' fits rather well for the course of a zodiacal sign in the precession of the equinoxes, and that, on the other hand, the number $540 = 77 \times 7 + 1$ has, like the number of the sevenfold 'week of years' of the jubilee ($50 = 7 \times 7 + 1$), of which it is so to speak an 'extension', a particular link with the septenary. In any case, these are almost the only detailed criticisms that we have to make this time, and the book as a whole is very worthy of interest and favorably distinguished from certain other works on cyclical theories which put forth far more ambitious and assuredly little justified claims. Naturally, he restricts himself to what we can call the 'minor historical cycles', and this only within the framework of the Western and Mediterranean civilizations; but we know that Georgel is presently preparing, in the same order of ideas, other works of a more general character, and we hope that he may soon be able to bring these also to a successful conclusion.

PART II

1

ATLANTIS
AND HYPERBOREA

In *Atlantis* (June 1929), Paul Le Cour comments on a footnote from
our article of last May,[1] in which we maintained the distinction
between Hyperborea and Atlantis against those who would conflate
them and speak of an 'Hyperborean Atlantis'. In truth, although this
expression seems to belong properly to Le Cour, our remarks were
not directed only at him, for he is not alone in confusing the two;
the same confusion can be found in Herman Wirth, author of an
important work on the origins of humanity (recently published in
Germany as *Der Aufgang der Menschheit*), who consistently uses the
term 'north-Atlantic' to designate the region from which the primordial tradition emerged. On the other hand, Le Cour is, to our
knowledge, the only one who claims that we affirm the existence of
an 'Hyperborean Atlantis'. If we did not single him out for this, it is
because questions of persons are of little importance to us, our only
concern being to put our readers on guard against a false interpretation, whatever its source may be. We wonder how Le Cour reads us;
we wonder more than ever, for he now has us saying that the North
Pole was originally 'not the one of today, but the adjoining region, it
seems, of Iceland and Greenland.' Where could he have found that?
We are absolutely certain that we have never written a single word
on this matter and that we have never made the slightest allusion to
the question, which is in any case secondary from our point of view,

1. This article, entitled 'Thunderbolts', appeared in the May 1929 issue of *Le Voile
d'Isis*, and forms chap. 27 of *Symbols of Sacred Science*.

of a possible displacement of the pole since the beginning of our *Manvantara*.[2] With all the more reason we have never specified its original location, which would be, in any event, on many grounds quite difficult to determine with respect to present-day regions.

Le Cour goes on to say that 'in spite of his [Guénon's] Hinduism, he admits that the origin of the traditions is Western.' We do not admit this at all, quite the contrary, for we say that it is polar, and as far as we know the pole is no more Western than it is Eastern; and we persist in maintaining, as we did in the note just referred to, that North and West are two different cardinal points. It is only in a later epoch that the seat of the primordial tradition, transferred to other regions, was able to become either Western or Eastern—Western for certain periods and Eastern for other; and in any case, the last trans-feral was surely to the East and already completed long before the beginning of the times called 'historic' (the only times accessible to the investigations of 'profane' history). We should note, moreover, that it is not at all 'in spite of his Hinduism' (in using this word Le Cour probably spoke more correctly than he knew), but on the con-trary because of it that we consider the origin of the traditions to be Nordic, and even more exactly to be polar, since this is expressly affirmed in the *Veda* as well as in other sacred books.[3] The land where the sun 'circled the horizon without setting' must have in fact been located very near the pole if not at the pole itself; it is also said that at a later date the representatives of the tradition were trans-ported to a region where the longest day was twice as long as the shortest, but this already involves a subsequent phase which, geo-graphically, clearly has nothing to do with Hyperborea.

Le Cour may be right in distinguishing between a southern Atlantis and a northern Atlantis, although they must not have been

2. This question seems to be linked to that of the inclination of the terrestrial axis, which, according to certain traditional ideas, would not have existed from the beginning, but was a consequence of what in Western language is called the 'Fall of Man'.

3. Those who want precise references here can find them in the remarkable work of B.G. Tilak, *The Arctic Home in the Veda*, which seems unfortunately to have remained completely unknown in Europe, no doubt because its author was a non-Westernized Hindu.

separate originally; but it is no less true that even the northern Atlantis had nothing hyperborean about it. As we freely acknowledge, what greatly complicates the issue is that over time the same designations have been applied to very different regions, and not only to successive locations of the traditional primordial center, but even to the secondary centers that proceeded more or less directly from it. We pointed out this difficulty in our study *The King of the World*, where, on the very page to which Le Cour refers, we wrote:

> But it is also necessary to distinguish the Atlantean *Tula* [the original place of the Toltecs, which was probably situated in Northern Atlantis] from the Hyperborean *Tula*, the latter then truly representing the original and supreme center for the totality of the present *Manvantara*; it was this that was the 'sacred isle' par excellence, having originally been situated quite literally at the pole.... All the other sacred isles, which everywhere bear names of identical meaning, were only its images; and this applies even to the spiritual center of the Atlantean tradition, which only presided over a secondary historical cycle subordinate to the *Manvantara*.

To which we added this note:

> A major difficulty in determining precisely the meeting-point of the Atlantean and the Hyperborean traditions results from various name substitutions that have given rise to many confusions; but in spite of everything the question is perhaps not entirely insoluble.[4]

---

4. [*The King of the World*, chap. 10, and note 2.] In regard to the Atlantean *Tula*, we think it worth reproducing here a piece of information that we gathered from a geography column in the *Journal des Debats* (January 22, 1929), entitled 'Les Indiens de l'isthme de Panama', whose importance certainly escaped even the author himself: 'In 1925, a great party of the Cuna Indians rose up, killed the Panamanian police that lived in their territory, and founded the Independent Republic of *Tulé*, whose flag was a *swastika* on an orange background with a red border. This republic still exists at the present time.' This seems to indicate that, in regard to the traditions of ancient America, much more still exists than one might be tempted to believe.

In speaking of this meeting-point, we were thinking chiefly of Druidism; and now, precisely on this subject, we find in *Atlantis* (July–August, 1929) another note that proves how difficult it sometimes is to make oneself understood. On the subject of our June article on the 'triple enclosure',[5] Le Cour writes: 'It limits the scope of this emblem to make it only a Druidic symbol; it is likely to be earlier and to radiate beyond the Druidic world.' Now we are so far from making it only a Druidic symbol that in our article, after having noted the examples Le Cour himself gathered from Italy and Greece, we said:

> The fact that this same figure is found elsewhere than among the Celts would indicate that there were, in other traditional forms, hierarchies constituted on this same model [of the Druidic hierarchy], which is perfectly normal.

As for the question of anteriority, it would be necessary first of all to know what precise epoch Druidism dates to, and it probably dates back earlier than is ordinarily supposed, all the more in that the Druids possessed a tradition of which a significant part was indisputably of hyperborean provenance.

We will take this occasion to make a further remark which has its own importance. We say 'hyperborean' to conform with the usage that has prevailed since the Greeks; but the use of this word shows that they, at least in the 'classical' epoch, had already lost the sense of the primitive designation. It would, in fact, suffice to say 'Boreas', a word strictly equivalent to the Sanskrit *Varāha*, or rather, when it involves an area of land, to its feminine form *Varahī*; it is the 'land of the wild boar', which also became the 'land of the bear' at a certain epoch during the period of ascendancy of the Kshatriyas, to which *Parashurāma*[6] put an end.

---

5. The article, entitled 'The Triple Enclosure of the Druids', appeared in *Le Voile d'Isis* in 1929, and forms chap. 12 of *Symbols of Sacred Science*.

6. This name *Varahī* is applied to the 'sacred land' and symbolically likened to a certain aspect of the *Shakti* of *Vishnu*, the latter then being envisaged especially in his third *avatāra*. There would be much to say on this subject, and perhaps we will someday return to it. This same name has never been used to designate Europe, as Saint Yves d'Alveydre seems to have believed; on the other hand, one might have

To finish this clarification, it remains for us to say a few words on three or four questions that Le Cour raises incidentally in his two notes. The first is a reference to the *swastika*, which he says we 'make the sign of the pole.' Without the slightest animosity, we will here ask Le Cour not to liken our case to his, for it is necessary to tell things as they are: we consider him a 'seeker' (and this is not in any way to lessen his merit) who offers explanations according to his personal views, which are somewhat adventurous at times; and that is altogether his right since he is not attached to any living tradition and is not in possession of any facts received by direct transmission. We could say, in other words, that he is doing archeology, whereas we are doing initiatic science, two points of view which, even when they touch upon the same subjects, cannot in any way coincide. We do not 'make' of the *swastika* the sign of the pole; we say that it is and has always been this, and that this is its true traditional meaning, which is an entirely different thing, for this is a fact that neither Le Cour nor we ourselves can change. Le Cour, who evidently can provide only more or less hypothetical interpretations, claims that the *swastika* is 'only a symbol related to an ideal lacking loftiness';[7] that is his way of seeing things, but it is nothing more than that, and so we are all the more reluctant to discuss it in that it represents only a sentimental opinion; 'lofty' or not, an 'ideal' is to us something rather empty, and in reality it is a question of things that are much more 'positive', as we would readily say if this word were not so abused.

Le Cour, on the other hand, does not appear satisfied with the note we devoted to an article by one of his collaborators who wished to see at all costs an opposition between East and West, and who

viewed these questions a little more clearly in the West if Fabre d'Olivet and those who followed him had not hopelessly entangled the story of *Parashurāma* with that of *Rāmachandra*, that is, the sixth and the seventh *avatāras*, who however are quite distinct in every respect.

7. We would suppose that in writing these words Le Cour had in mind modern and not traditional interpretations of the *swastika*, like those conceived by the German 'racists', for example, who in effect claimed to take possession of this emblem, dressing it up, moreover, with the baroque and trivial appellation of *hakenkreuz*, or 'hooked cross'.

showed, with regard to the East, an altogether deplorable exclusivism.[8] He writes some astonishing things concerning this:

> René Guénon, who is a pure logician, can only investigate the purely intellectual side of things, concerning the East as well as the West, as is proven by his writings; he demonstrates this again in declaring that *Agni* is sufficient unto itself (see *Regnabit*, April 1926), and in ignoring the duality *Aor-Agni*, to which we will often return, for this duality is the cornerstone of the edifice of the manifested world.

Although we are ordinarily indifferent to what is written about us, we cannot let it pass that we are a 'pure logician' when on the contrary we consider logic and dialectic to be simple expository instruments, as such useful at times, but of an entirely external character and without any interest in themselves. To repeat, we adhere only to the initiatic point of view, and the rest, that is to say all that is only 'profane' knowledge, is entirely without value in our eyes. Although we often do speak of 'pure intellectuality', it is only because this expression has a completely different meaning for us than it does for Le Cour, who seems to confuse 'intelligence' with 'reason' and who even envisages an 'esthetic intuition', whereas there is no genuine intuition other than 'intellectual intuition', which is of a suprarational order. There is here, moreover, something formidable in quite another way than can be conceived by one who clearly has not the least suspicion of what 'metaphysical realization' might be, and who probably imagines that we are only a kind of theoretician, which proves once more that he has scarcely understood our writings, which, strange to say, nonetheless appear to preoccupy him.

As for the fable of *Aor-Agni*, of which we are not in the least 'ignorant', it would be good once and for all to make an end of these reveries, for which Le Cour is moreover not responsible: if '*Agni* is sufficient unto itself', it is for the good reason that in Sanskrit this

---

8. Le Cour reproaches us for having said that his collaborator 'certainly does not have the gift of languages,' which he finds 'an unfortunate statement'; alas, he quite simply confuses the 'gift of languages' with linguistic knowledge, whereas what is involved has absolutely nothing to do with erudition.

term designates fire in all its aspects, and those who claim the contrary demonstrate their total ignorance of Hindu tradition. We did not say anything other than this in the note in our *Regnabit* article, which we believe it necessary to reproduce here:

> Knowing that among the readers of *Regnabit* there are some who are acquainted with the theories of a school whose works, though very interesting and quite admirable in many respects, nonetheless invite certain reservations, we must say here that we cannot accept the use of the terms *Aor* and *Agni* to designate the two complementary aspects of fire (light and heat). The first of these two words is in fact Hebrew, while the second is Sanskrit, and one cannot associate in this way terms borrowed from different traditions, whatever may be, among such traditions, the real concordances and even the fundamental identity hidden under their diversity of forms; we must not confuse 'syncretism' with true synthesis. Moreover, if *Aor* is exclusively light, *Agni* is the igneous principle envisaged integrally (the Latin *ignis* being exactly the same word), and therefore light and heat together; the restriction of this term to the second aspect is entirely arbitrary and unjustified.

We need hardly add that in writing this note we in no way had Le Cour in mind; we were thinking solely of Hiéron de Paray-le-Monial, to whom the invention of this bizarre verbal association properly belongs. We see no reason to give any attention to a fantasy issuing from Sarachaga's too fertile imagination, entirely lacking in authority and without the slightest value from the traditional point of view, to which we strictly confine ourselves.[9]

Finally, Le Cour takes advantage of these circumstances to affirm once again the anti-metaphysical and anti-initiatic theory of Western 'individualism', which is after all his own concern and involves only himself; and he adds, with a note of pride indicating quite well that he is hardly free from individual contingencies: 'We maintain

---

9. This is the same Sarachaga who wrote *zwadisca* for *swastika*; one of his disciples, to whom we once made this observation, assured us that he must have had a reason for writing it thus—a justification we find a little too facile!

our point of view because we are ancestors in the domain of knowledge.' This claim is truly a little extraordinary—does Le Cour then
believe himself to be so ancient? Not only are modern Westerners
not the ancestors of anyone, they are not even legitimate descendants, for they have lost the key to their own tradition; it is not 'in
the East that there has been deviation,' whatever might be said by
those who are ignorant of everything pertaining to the Eastern doctrines. The 'ancestors', to take up Le Cour's word, are the effective
holders of the primordial tradition; there could not be any others,
and, in the present age, these will certainly not be found in the West.

2

THE PLACE OF THE
ATLANTEAN TRADITION
IN THE *MANVANTARA*

IN THE PRECEDING CHAPTER we pointed out the all too common confusion between the primordial tradition, which was originally 'polar' in the literal sense of the word and whose starting-point is the very same as the present *Manvantara*, and the derivative and secondary Atlantean tradition, which relates to a much more restricted period. We said then, as we have said before,[1] that this confusion could be explained in some measure by the fact that the subordinate spiritual centers were constituted in the image of the supreme center, and that the same appellations had been applied to them. Thus it is that the Atlantean *Tula*, a name preserved in Central America where it was brought by the Toltecs, must have been the seat of a spiritual power that was as it were an emanation from that of the Hyperborean *Tula*; and since the name *Tula* designates Libra [the Scales], its double application is closely related to the transfer of that same designation from the polar constellation of the Great Bear to the zodiacal sign which even today bears the name of the Scales. It is also to the Atlantean tradition that one should relate the transfer of the *sapta-riksha* (the symbolic dwelling place of the seven *Rishis*) at a certain epoch from the same Great Bear to the Pleiades, a constellation also formed of seven stars but in a zodiacal position; what leaves no doubt in this respect is that the Pleiades were said to be daughters of Atlas and, as such, also called Atlantides.

1. See particularly *The King of the World*.

All this is in accord with the geographical locations of the traditional centers, themselves linked to their own characteristics as well as to their respective places in the cyclical period, for everything here holds together more closely than could be supposed by those ignorant of the laws of certain correspondences. Hyperborea obviously corresponds to the North, and Atlantis to the West; and it is remarkable that although the very designations of these two regions are clearly distinct, they may also give rise to confusion since names of the same root were applied to both. In fact, one finds this root under diverse forms such as *hiber*, *iber*, or *eber*, and also *ereb* by transposition of letters, designating both the region of winter, that is, the North, and the region of evening or the setting sun, that is, the West, and the peoples who inhabit both; this fact is manifestly of the same order as those we just mentioned.

The very position of the Atlantean center on the East-West axis indicates its subordination with respect to the Hyperborean center, located at the North-South polar axis. Indeed, although in the complete system of the six directions of space the conjunction of these two axes forms what one can call a horizontal cross, the North-South axis must nonetheless be regarded as relatively vertical with respect to the East-West axis, as we have explained elsewhere.[2] In conformity with the symbolism of the annual cycle, one can still call the first of these two axes the solstitial axis and the second the equinoctial axis; and this helps us understand that the starting-point given to the year may not be the same in all the traditional forms. The starting-point that one can call normal, as being in direct conformity with primordial tradition, is the winter solstice; the fact of starting the year at one of the equinoxes indicates the attachment to a secondary tradition, such as the Atlantean tradition.

Since this last, on the other hand, is located in a region that corresponds to evening in the diurnal cycle, it must be regarded as belonging to one of the last divisions of the cycle of present terrestrial humanity and therefore as relatively recent; and in fact, without seeking to give precise details which would be difficult to justify, one can say that it certainly belongs to the second half of the present

2. See our study *The Symbolism of the Cross.*

Manvantara.[3] Besides, just as the autumn of the year corresponds to evening in the day, one can see a direct allusion to the Atlantean world in the fact that the Hebraic tradition (whose name moreover betrays its Western origin) indicates that the world was created at the autumn equinox (the first day of the month of *Thishri* according to a certain transposition of the word *Bereshith*); and perhaps that is also the most immediate reason (there are others of a more profound order) for the enunciation of 'evening' (*ereb*) before 'morning' (*boker*) in the recital of the 'days' of Genesis.[4] This is confirmed by the fact that the literal meaning of the name Adam is 'red', for the Atlantean tradition was precisely that of the red race; and it seems also that the biblical deluge corresponds directly to the cataclysm in which Atlantis disappeared and that, consequently, it must not be identified with the deluge of *Satyavrata* which, according to Hindu tradition, having issued directly from the primordial tradition, immediately preceded the beginning of our *Manvantara*.[5] Of course, this meaning, which one can call historical, does not in any way exclude the other meanings; besides, one must never lose sight of the fact that, according to the analogy that exists between a principal cycle and the secondary cycles into which it is subdivided, all considerations of this order are always susceptible of applications at different degrees; but what we wish to say is that, although the Atlantean cycle was taken as a foundation in the Hebrew tradition, it seems that the transmission was made either by the mediation of the Egyptians—which at least has nothing improbable about it—or by altogether different means.

---

3. We think that the duration of the Atlantean civilization must have been equal to a 'great year' understood in the sense of the half-period of the precession of the equinoxes; as to the cataclysm that put an end to it, certain concordant data seem to indicate that it took place 7,200 years before the year 720 of the *Kali-Yuga*, a year which is itself the starting-point of a known era, but of which those who still use it today no longer seem to know the origin or the significance.

4. Among the Arabs, too, the custom is to count the hours of the day beginning with the *maghreb*, that is, the setting of the sun.

5. On the other hand, the deluges of *Deucalion* and *Ogyges* among the Greeks, seem to relate to periods even more limited and to partial cataclysms later than that of Atlantis.

If we make this last reservation, it is because it seems particularly difficult to determine how, after the disappearance of Atlantis, the current coming from the West was joined with another current descending from the North and proceeding directly from the primordial tradition, a junction from which was to result the constitution of the different traditional forms proper to the last part of the *Manvantara*. This is in any case not a matter of a reabsorption pure and simple in the primordial tradition of what went forth from it at an earlier epoch; it is a matter of a sort of fusion of forms previously differentiated to give birth to other forms adapted to new circumstances of time and place; and the fact that the two currents then appear in a way to be autonomous can further support the illusion of the independence of the Atlantean tradition. If one wished to research the conditions under which that fusion took place, it would doubtless be necessary to give particular importance to the Celts and the Chaldeans, whose name, which is the same, designated in reality not a particular people, but rather a sacerdotal caste; but who knows today what the Celtic and Chaldean traditions were, or even that of the ancient Egyptians? One cannot be overprudent when it comes to civilizations that have entirely disappeared, and it is certainly not the attempts at reconstitution to which profane archeologists devote themselves that are likely to shed light on the question; but it is nonetheless true that many vestiges of a forgotten past are coming out of the earth in our age, and perhaps not without reason. Without risking the slightest prediction on what can result from these discoveries, the possible importance of which those who make them are generally incapable of suspecting, we must certainly see in this a 'sign of the times'. Must not everything be found again at the end of the *Manvantara*, to serve as a starting-point for the elaboration of the future cycle?

PART III

1

A FEW REMARKS
ON THE NAME *ADAM*

IN THE LAST CHAPTER we said that the literal meaning of the name *Adam* is 'red', and that one can see in it one indication of the link of the Hebraic tradition to the Atlantean tradition, which was that of the red race. On the other hand, in his interesting article on 'blood and some of its mysteries', our colleague Argos envisages for this same name *Adam* a derivation that may seem different. After recalling the usual interpretation that it means 'drawn from the earth' (*adamah*), he asks whether it could not rather come from the word *dam*, 'blood'; but the difference is only apparent, since all these words really have one and the same root.

It is worth remarking first of all that from the linguistic point of view the usual etymology, which derives *Adam* from *adamah*, translated as 'earth', is impossible; the inverse derivation would be more plausible, but in fact the two substantives both come from the same verbal root *adam*, which means 'to be red'. *Adamah* is not, originally at least, the earth in general (*eretz*) or the element earth (*yabashah*, a word whose original meaning indicates 'dryness' as a quality characteristic of this element). It is properly red clay, which by its plastic properties is particularly apt to represent a certain potentiality, a capacity to receive forms; and the work of the potter has often been taken as a symbol of the production of manifested beings from the undifferentiated primordial substance. It is for the same reason that 'red earth' seems to have special importance in Hermetic symbolism, where it can be taken for one of the symbols of 'prime matter', although when understood in its literal sense it can only play that role in a very relative way since it is already endowed with definite qualities. Let us add that the relationship between a designation of the earth and the name of *Adam*, taken as a type of humanity, is found in another form in Latin, where the word *humus*, 'earth', is also singularly close to *homo* and *humanus*. On the other hand, if we relate this same name *Adam* more particularly to the tradition of the red race, the latter corresponds, among the elements, to earth, as it does to the West among the cardinal points, and this last concordance further justifies what we said previously.

As for the word *dam*, 'blood' (which is common to Hebrew and Arabic), it is also derived from the same root *adam:*[1] blood is properly the red fluid, which is in fact its most immediately apparent characteristic. The kinship between this designation of blood and the name of *Adam* is therefore incontestable and is self-evident through derivation from a common root; but this derivation appears to be direct for both, and it is not possible, starting from the verbal root *adam*, to pass by way of the intermediary of *dam* to the name of *Adam*. One could, it is true, envisage things in another way, less strictly linguistic, and say that it is because of his blood that man is called 'red'. Such an explanation is not very satisfying because the fact of having blood is not confined to man but is common with the animal species, so that it cannot really serve to characterize him. In fact in Hermetic symbolism the color red is that of the animal kingdom, as the color green is that of the vegetable kingdom and the color white that of the mineral kingdom;[2] and this, as regards the color red, can be related precisely to blood considered as the seat, or rather the support, of animal vitality properly speaking. From another point of view, if one comes back to the more specific relation of the name of *Adam* with the red race, the latter does not seem [in spite of its color] susceptible of being related to a predominance of blood in its organic constitution, for the sanguine temperament corresponds to fire among the elements, and not to earth;

---

1. The initial *aleph*, which exists in the root, disappears in the derived word, which is not an exceptional fact. This *aleph* does not in any way constitute a prefix having an independent meaning, as is thought by Latouche, whose linguistic conceptions are too often fanciful.

2. On the symbolism of these three colors, see our study *The Esoterism of Dante*.

and it is the black race which corresponds to the element of *fire*, as it does to the *South* among the cardinal points.

Let us further point out that among the derivatives of the root *Adam* is the word *edom*, which means 'reddish-brown' and which in any case differs from the name of *Adam* only by vowel points. In the Bible, *Edom* is a surname of Esau, whence the name 'Edomites' given to his descendants, and that of Idumaea to the country they inhabited (and which in Hebrew is also *Edom*, but in the feminine). This recalls the 'seven kings of Edom' mentioned in the *Zohar*, and the close resemblance of *Edom* to *Adam* may be one of the reasons why this name is taken here to designate the vanished peoples, that is, those of the previous *Manvantaras*.[3] We also see the relationship that this last point presents with the question of what has been called the 'pre-adamites': if one takes *Adam* as being the origin of the red race and of its particular tradition, it can simply be a matter of the other races that have preceded the former in the course of the present human cycle. If we take it in a more extended sense as the prototype for the whole of present humanity, it will be a case of these earlier humanities to which precisely the 'seven kings of Edom' refers. In all cases, the discussions to which this question has given rise appear to be quite vain, for there should not be any difficulty about it, and in fact there is none, at least for the Islamic tradition, in which there exists an *ḥadith* (saying of the Prophet) that 'before the Adam whom we know, God created a hundred thousand Adams' (that is, an undetermined number), which is as clear an affirmation as can be of the multiplicity of the cyclical periods and of the corresponding humanities.

Since we alluded to blood as the support of vitality, we will recall that, as we have already had occasion to explain in one of our works,[4] the blood effectively constitutes one of the links of the corporeal organism with the subtle state of the living being, which is properly the 'soul' (the *nephesh chayah* ['living soul'] of Genesis), that is, in the etymological sense (*anima*), the principal animator or

---

3. See *The King of the World*, end of chap. 6.

4. *Man and His Becoming according to the Vedānta*, chap. 14. Cf. also *The Spiritist Fallacy*, pp 116–119.

vivifying force of the being. The subtle state is called *Taijasa* in the Hindu tradition, by analogy with *tejas* or the igneous element; and as fire is qualitatively polarized into light and heat, the subtle state is linked to the corporeal state in two different and complementary ways: through the blood as to the caloric quality and through the nervous system as to the luminous quality. In fact, even simply from the physiological point of view, blood is the vehicle of animating heat; and this explains the correspondence we indicated above of the sanguine temperament with the element fire. On the other hand, one can say that, in fire, light represents the superior aspect and heat the inferior aspect: Islamic tradition teaches that angels were created from the 'divine fire' (or from the 'divine light'), and that those who rebelled as followers of *Iblis* lost their natural luminosity, retaining only a lowly heat.[5] Consequently, one can say that the blood is directly related to the inferior aspect of the subtle state; and from this comes the interdiction of blood as nourishment, since its absorption conveys that which is grossest in animal vitality, and which, being assimilated and mingling intimately with the psychic elements of man, can actually have very serious consequences. From this also derives the frequent use of blood in the practices of magic and even of sorcery (as attracting the 'infernal' entities by similarity of nature). But on the other hand, this is also susceptible under certain conditions of a transposition to a superior order, whence derive rites, either religious or even initiatic (like the Mithraic 'taurobolus' [bull sacrifice]), involving animal sacrifices; and since in this respect it is said that the sacrifice of Abel is opposed to the unbloody sacrifice of Cain, we will perhaps return to this point on some future occasion.

5. This is indicated in the relationship which exists in Arabic between the words *nūr*, 'light' and *nār*, 'fire' (in the sense of heat).

2

KABBALAH

THE TERM *Kabbalah*[1] in Hebrew means nothing else than 'tradition' in the most general sense, and although it generally designates the esoteric or initiatic tradition when used with no further precision, it also sometimes happens that it may be applied to the exoteric tradition itself.[2] This term can therefore designate any tradition; but since it belongs to the Hebraic language, it is normal to reserve it to the Hebrew tradition alone, as we have noted on other occasions, or, if one prefers perhaps a more exact way of speaking, to the specifically Hebrew form of the tradition. If we insist on this point, it is because we have noted that some people have a tendency to attach another meaning to this word, to make it the name of a special type of traditional knowledge, wherever this may be found, and this because they believe they have discovered in the word all sorts of more or less extraordinary things that really are not there at all. We do not intend to waste our time bringing up all these fanciful interpretations; it is more useful to clarify the original meaning of the word, which will suffice to reduce them to nothing, and this is all we propose to do here.

The root QBL in Hebrew and Arabic[3] signifies essentially the relationship of two things placed face to face with one another, and

1. Although the initial 'K' has been retained in spelling *Kabbalah*, since this represents current practice, when other terms and roots are introduced, the letter 'Q' has been used, as in the original French and in common philological practice. ED.

2. This has not failed to cause certain errors: thus, we have seen some claim to link the *Talmud* to the 'Kabbalah', understood in the esoteric sense; indeed, the *Talmud* is certainly from the 'tradition', but is purely exoteric, religious, and legal.

3. We call attention to the fact, which perhaps is not sufficiently noticed, that these two languages, which share most of their roots, can very often shed light on one another.

from this come all the varied meanings of the words derived from it, as for example those of encounter and even opposition. From this relationship also comes the idea of a passage from the one to the other of the two terms, whence ideas like those of receiving, welcoming, and accepting expressed in the two languages through the verb *qabal*; and *Kabbalah* derives directly from this, that is to say 'that which is received' or transmitted (in Latin *traditum*) from one to the other. Here there appears, along with the idea of transmission, that of a succession; but it must be noted that the primary meaning of the root indicates a relationship that can be simultaneous as well as successive, spatial as well as temporal. And this explains the double meaning of the preposition *qabal* in Hebrew and *qabl* in Arabic, which signify both 'in front of' (that is, 'facing' in space) and 'before' (in time); and the close relationship of these two words, 'in front of' and 'before', even in French,[4] clearly shows that there is always a certain analogy between these two different modalities, one in simultaneity and the other in succession. This also allows the resolution of an apparent contradiction: although the usual idea when it comes to a temporal relationship is that of anteriority, which relates therefore to the past, it also happens that derivatives from the same root designate the future (in Arabic *mustaqbal*, that is to say literally that toward which one goes, from *istaqbal*, 'to go toward'). But do we not also say in French that the past is 'before' [*avant*] us, and the future is 'in front of' [*devant*] us, which is quite comparable? In sum, it suffices in every case that one of the two terms considered be 'in front of' or 'before' the other, whether it be a question of a spatial relationship or a temporal one.

All these remarks can be further confirmed by the examination of another root, equally common to Hebrew and Arabic, and which has meanings very close to these, one could even say identical in great part, for even though their starting-point is clearly different the derived meanings converge. This is the root QDM, which in the first place expresses the idea of 'to precede' (*qadam*), whence all that refers not only to a temporal anteriority but to a priority of any order. Thus for words derived from this root one finds, besides the

---

4. In French, *devant* and *avant*. ED.

original and ancient meanings (*qedem* in Hebrew, *qidm* or *qidam* in Arabic) that of primacy or precedence and even that of walking, advancing, or progression (in Arabic *taqaddum*);[5] and here again, the preposition *qadam* in Hebrew and *quddam* in Arabic has the double meaning of 'in front of' and 'before'. But the principal meaning designates what is first, whether hierarchically or chronologically; thus the idea most frequently expressed is that of origin or primordiality, and by extension, that of antiquity when the temporal order is involved. Thus, *qadmon* in Hebrew and *qadim* in Arabic signify 'ancient' in current usage, but when they are related to the domain of principles, they must be translated by 'primordial'.[6]

Concerning these same words, there are other reasons that are not without interest. In Hebrew, derivatives of the root QDM also serve to designate the East,[7] that is, the direction of the 'origin' in the sense that it is there that the rising sun appears (*oriens*, from *oriri*, from which comes also *origo* in Latin), the starting-point of the diurnal course of the sun; and at the same time it is also the point used when 'orienting' oneself by turning toward the rising sun.[8] Thus *qedem* also means 'East', and *qadmon* 'eastern'; but one should not see in these designations the affirmation of a primordiality of the East from the point of view of the history of terrestrial humanity, since, as we have often said, the original tradition is Nordic, 'polar' even, and neither Eastern nor Western; moreover, the

5. From which comes the word *qadam*, meaning 'foot', that is, what serves for walking.

6. *Al-insān al-qadim*, that is, 'primordial Man' is, in Arabic, one of the designations of 'Universal Man' (synonym of *Al-insān al-kāmil*, which is literally 'perfect or complete Man'); it is precisely the Hebraic *Adam Qadmon*.

7. In French, *Orient*, whence *oriental*, 'eastern'. As pointed out below, the Latin *oriri* means 'to rise'. ED.

8. It is curious to note that Christ is sometimes called *Oriens*, a designation that can doubtless be related to the symbolism of the rising sun; but by reason of the double meaning we are indicating here it is possible that we should also, and even above all, relate it to the Hebrew *Elohi Qedem* or the expression designating the Word as the 'Ancient of Days', that is, He who is before the days, or the Principle of the cycles of manifestation represented symbolically as 'days' by various traditions (the 'days of Brahmā' in the Hindu tradition, the 'days of the creation' in the Hebrew Genesis).

explanation we just indicated seems to us fully sufficient. We will add in this connection that these questions of 'orientation' are generally quite important in traditional symbolism and in rites based on that symbolism; they are, besides, more complex than one might think and can give rise to certain errors, for in the different traditional forms there are many different modes of orientation. When one turns toward the rising sun, as we have just said, the South is designated as the 'right side' (*yamīn* or *yaman*; cf. the Sanskrit *dakshina*, which has the same meaning) and the North as the 'left side' (*shemōl* in Hebrew, *shimāl* in Arabic); but it also happens that orientation is established by turning toward the sun at the meridian, and the point before one is then no longer the East but the South. Thus in Arabic the South has among other names that of *qiblah*, and the adjective *qibli* means 'southern' [*meridional*]. These last terms bring us to the root QBL; the same word *qiblah* is also known in Islam to designate the ritual orientation; in all cases it is the direction one has in front of one; and what is also rather curious is that the spelling of the word *qiblah* is exactly identical to that of the Hebrew *qabbalah*.

Now, one can ask why it is that in Hebrew 'tradition' is designated by a word coming from the root QBL, and not from the root QDM. It is tempting to answer that since the Hebrew tradition constitutes only a secondary and derived form, a name evoking the idea of origin or primordiality would not be fitting; but this argument does not seem to us to be essential, for directly or not, every tradition is linked to its origins and proceeds from the primordial tradition, and we have even seen elsewhere that every sacred language, including Hebrew itself and Arabic, is thought to represent the primordial language in some way. The real reason, it seems, is that the idea that must especially be highlighted here is that of a regular and uninterrupted transmission, which is therefore properly expressed by the word 'tradition', as we noted at the beginning. This transmission constitutes the 'chain' (*shelsheleth* in Hebrew, *silsilah* in Arabic) that unites the present to the past and that must continue from the present into the future; it is the 'chain of tradition' (*shelsheleth ha-qabbalah*) or the 'initiatic chain' which we recently had occasion to speak of; and it is also the determination of a 'direction' (we find here the meaning of the Arabic *qiblah*) which, through the course of time, orients the cycle toward its end and joins it again with its origin, and which, extending even beyond these two extreme points by the fact that its principial source is timeless and 'non-human', links it harmoniously to the other cycles, forming with these a greater 'chain', that which certain Eastern traditions call the 'chain of worlds' into which by degrees is integrated the entire order of universal manifestation.

3

KABBALAH AND
THE SCIENCE OF NUMBERS

WE HAVE OFTEN STRESSED the fact that the 'sacred sciences' belonging to a given traditional form are really an integral part of it, at least as secondary and subordinate elements, and are far from representing merely a kind of adventitious addition linked to it more or less artificially. It is indispensable to understand this point well and never to lose sight of it if we wish to penetrate, however little, into the true spirit of a tradition; and it is all the more necessary to call attention to this, as in our day one rather frequently notes among those who claim to study traditional doctrines a tendency not to take these sciences into account, either because of the special difficulties presented by their assimilation, or because, in addition to the impossibility of fitting them into the framework of modern classifications, their presence is particularly annoying for anyone who strives to reduce everything to exoteric points of view and interprets doctrines in terms of 'philosophy' or 'mysticism'. Without wishing to elaborate yet again on the futility of such studies undertaken 'from the outside' and with wholly profane intentions, we will nevertheless repeat, because we see daily the opportunity, that the distorted ideas to which they inevitably lead are certainly worse than pure and simple ignorance.

It sometimes even happens that certain traditional sciences play a more important role than that we have just indicated, and that apart from the proper value they possess in themselves in their contingent order, they are taken as symbolic means of expression for the higher and essential part of the doctrine, to the extent that this becomes entirely unintelligible if we try to separate it from them. This is what happens in particular with the Hebrew Kabbalah for the 'science of numbers', which moreover is largely identical to the 'science of let-ters', just as it is in Islamic esoterism, and this in virtue of the very constitution of the Hebrew and Arabic languages, which as we have just said are so close to one another in all respects.[1]

The preponderant role of the science of numbers in the Kabbalah is a fact so evident that it cannot escape even the most superficial observer, and it is hardly possible even for 'critics' who are most full of prejudice or bias, to deny or to conceal it. Nevertheless, they are not remiss in giving erroneous interpretations of this fact in order to somehow make it fit into the framework of their preconceived ideas; we propose here especially to dissipate these more or less deliberate confusions, due in good part to abuse of the too famous 'historical method', which in spite of everything wants to see 'bor-rowings' anywhere it sees similarities.

We know that it is fashionable in university circles to claim that the Kabbalah is linked to Neoplatonism, so as to diminish both its antiquity and its scope; is it not considered to be an unquestionable principle that everything must come from the Greeks? It is unfortu-nately forgotten that Neoplatonism itself contains many elements that are not specifically Greek, and that in the Alexandrian period Judaism in particular had a far from negligible importance, so that if there really were borrowings, they could have occurred in a direc-tion opposite to that claimed. This hypothesis is even more likely, first because the adoption of a foreign doctrine is hardly reconcil-able with the 'particularism' that was always one of the dominant traits of the Judaic spirit, and then because, whatever one may think in other respects of Neoplatonism, it represents only a relatively exoteric doctrine (even if it is based on esoteric ideas, it is only an 'exteriorization' of them), which as such has not been able to exer-cise a real influence on an essentially initiatic and even very 'closed' tradition such as Kabbalah is and always has been.[2] Besides, we do

1. See the chapter 'Kabbalah' above; we ask our readers to refer also to the study 'The Science of Letters', which forms chapter 8 of *Symbols of Sacred Science*.

2. This last argument is equally valid against the claim of linking Islamic esoter-ism to the same Neoplatonism. Among the Arabs, only philosophy is of Greek ori-gin, as is the case wherever we meet it with everything to which the name of philosophy (in Arabic, *falsafah*) can properly be applied, this name being as it were a mark of this origin; but here philosophy is no longer involved at all.

not see that there is any particularly striking resemblance between this and Neoplatonism, nor do we see in the form in which Neoplatonism is expressed that numbers play the same role that is so characteristic of the Kabbalah. The Greek language would hardly have allowed it, while it is, we repeat, something inherent to the Hebrew language itself, and must consequently have been linked from the beginning to the traditional form that expresses itself by it.

There is of course no reason to dispute that a traditional science of numbers may have existed among the Greeks, for it was as we know the basis of Pythagorism, which was not only a philosophy but also had a properly initiatic character; and it is from this that Plato drew not only the entire cosmological part of his doctrine such as expounded particularly in the *Timaeus*, but even his 'theory of ideas', which is really only a transposition in different terminology of the Pythagorean ideas about numbers considered as the principles of things. If we really want to find among the Greeks a term of comparison with the Kabbalah we must turn to Pythagorism; but it is precisely here that the inanity of the thesis of 'borrowings' becomes most clearly apparent. We are indeed in the presence of two initiatic doctrines, both of which give primary importance to the science of numbers, but that science is presented by each under radically different forms.

Here, some considerations of a more general order will be worthwhile. It is perfectly normal that the same science should be found in different traditions, for truth in any domain could not be the monopoly of one traditional form to the exclusion of others. This fact cannot then be a cause for astonishment except no doubt for the 'critics', who do not believe in the truth; and indeed it is the contrary that would be, not only surprising, but even scarcely conceivable. There is nothing here that implies a more or less direct communication between two different traditions, even in the case where one is incontestably more ancient than the other; can a certain truth not be seen and expressed independently of those who have already expressed it before, and, given that independence, is it not all the more probable that this same truth will in fact be expressed differently? It must however be clearly understood that this is in no way contrary to the common origin of all traditions;

but the transmission of principles from this common origin does not necessarily imply the explicit transmission of all the developments that are implicit in it and all the applications which they can produce. All that is a matter of 'adaptation', in a word, can be considered to belong properly to this or that particular traditional form, and, if one finds the equivalent elsewhere, that is because from the same principles one would naturally draw the same conclusions, whatever be the special way in which they will have been expressed here or there (with the reservation of course that certain symbolic modes of expression, being everywhere the same, must be regarded as going back to the primordial tradition). Moreover, the differences of form will generally be greater as one moves further away from principles to descend to more contingent orders; and this is one of the main difficulties in understanding certain traditional sciences.

It is easy to understand that these considerations remove almost all interest regarding the origin of the traditions or the provenance of the elements which they contain according to the 'historical' point of view as understood in the profane world, since they render perfectly useless the supposition of any direct filiation; and even where one notes a much closer similarity between two traditional forms, that similarity is explained far less by 'borrowings', which are often quite unlikely, than by 'affinities' due to a certain ensemble of common or similar conditions (race, type of language, way of life, etc.) among the peoples to whom these forms respectively apply.[3] As

3. This can be applied particularly to the similarity of expression we have already pointed out between the *Kabbalah* and Islamic esoterism. Regarding this last point there is a rather curious remark to make: its 'exoterist' adversaries, in Islam itself, have often tried to deprecate it by attributing to it a foreign origin; and under the pretext that many of the best-known *Sufis* were Persian, they claim to see in it borrowings from Mazdaism, even extending this gratuitous affirmation to the 'science of letters'. Now, there is no trace of anything at all like this among the ancient Persians, whereas this science exists on the contrary in a very similar form in Judaism, something that is explained very simply by the 'affinities' to which we alluded, not to mention the more remote community of origin to which we will have to return. But even though this fact is perhaps the only one that could give some appearance of likelihood to the idea of a borrowing from a pre-Islamic and non-Arabic doctrine, it seems to have totally escaped them!

for cases of real filiation, this is not to say that they must be entirely excluded, for it is evident that all traditional forms do not proceed directly from the primordial tradition and that other forms must have sometimes played the role of intermediaries; but the latter are most often traditions that have entirely disappeared, and those transmissions in general go back to epochs far too distant for ordinary history—whose field of investigation is really very limited—to be capable of the slightest knowledge of them, not counting the fact that the means by which they were effected are not among those accessible to its methods of research.

All of this only seems to take us away from our subject, and so returning now to the relationships between the Kabbalah and Pythagorism, we can now ask ourselves this question: if the former cannot be derived directly from the latter (even supposing that it is not anterior to it), and even if this is only because of too great a difference in form, something to which we will return presently in a more precise fashion, can one not at least envisage a common origin for both, which according to some would be the tradition of the ancient Egyptians (this of course would take us back well before the Alexandrian period)? Let us say right away that this is a theory that has been much abused; and as concerns Judaism, we are unable in spite of certain more or less fanciful assertions to discover the slightest connection with what is known of the Egyptian tradition (we are speaking here of the form, the only thing to be considered, since the substance is necessarily identical in all traditions); doubtless it would have links that are more real with the Chaldean tradition, whether by derivation or by simple affinity, as far as it is possible to really grasp something of these traditions that have been extinct for so many centuries.

As for Pythagorism, the question is perhaps more complex. The journeys of Pythagoras, whether they are to be taken literally or symbolically, do not necessarily imply borrowings from doctrines of this or that people (at least as to the essentials, whatever may be the case for certain points of detail), but rather the establishment or strengthening of certain links with more or less equivalent initiations. It seems that Pythagorism in fact was above all the continuation of something that existed earlier in Greece itself, and that there is no reason to look elsewhere for its principal source; we have in mind the Mysteries, and more particularly Orphism, of which it was perhaps only a 'readaptation' in this epoch of the sixth century before the Christian era, which by a strange synchronism saw changes of form take place at once among almost all peoples. It is often said that the Greek Mysteries were themselves of Egyptian origin, but such a general assertion is much too 'simplistic', and although this may be true in certain cases such as the Mysteries of Eleusis (which particularly come to mind in the circumstances), there are others where this is not tenable at all.[4] Whether it be a question of Pythagorism itself or the earlier Orphism, it is not at Eleusis that we must look for the 'connecting point', but at Delphi; and the Delphic Apollo is not at all Egyptian but Hyperborean, an origin which is in any case impossible to envisage for the Hebrew tradition.[5] And this leads us directly to the most important point as regards the science of numbers and the different forms it has assumed.

This science of numbers in Pythagorism appears closely linked to that of geometric forms; and it is the same in Plato, who in this respect is purely Pythagorean. One could see here the expression of a characteristic trait of the Hellenistic mentality, which is especially tied to visual forms; and we know that among the mathematical sciences it is in fact geometry that the Greeks especially developed.[6] However, there is something else involved here, at least as regards 'sacred geometry'; the 'geometer' God of Pythagoras and Plato, understood in its most precise and, we could say, technical meaning,

---

4. It is hardly necessary to say that certain stories in which Moses and Orpheus both receive initiation at the same time in the temples of Egypt are only fantasies with no serious basis; and what has not been said on Egyptian initiation since Abbé Terrasson's *Séthos*?

5. We are speaking here of direct derivation. Even if the primordial tradition is Hyperborean, and if consequently all traditional forms without exception are in the end linked to that origin, there are cases like that of the Hebrew tradition where this could only be very indirectly and through a long series of intermediaries, which would moreover be very difficult to reconstruct exactly.

6. Algebra, on the other hand, is of Indian origin, and was only introduced into the West much later by the Arabs, who gave to it the name it has retained (*al-jabr*).

is none other than Apollo. We cannot undertake an elaboration of this subject, which would lead us too far afield, and we may perhaps come back to this question on another occasion. It is enough at present to point out that this fact is sharply opposed to the hypothesis of a common origin for both Pythagorism and the Kabbalah, even on the very point where a special effort has been made to link them, and which is really the only point which could have raised the idea of such a connection, that is, the apparent similarity between the two doctrines with regard to the role the science of numbers plays in them.

In the Kabbalah this same science of numbers is in not at all connected to geometric symbolism in the same way; and it is easy to see that this should be so, for this symbolism could not be suitable for nomadic peoples such as the Hebrews and the Arabs originally were.[7] On the other hand, we find something there which does not have its equivalent among the Greeks: the close union, one could even say the identity in many respects, of the science of numbers with that of letters by reason of the latter's numerical correspondences. This is what is eminently characteristic of the Kabbalah[8] and is found nowhere else, at least under this aspect and with this development, unless, as we have already said, it be in Islamic esoterism, that is to say in the Arabic tradition.

It might seem surprising at first sight that considerations of this kind should have remained foreign to the Greeks,[9] since their letters

7. On this point, see chapter 21 of *The Reign of Quantity and The Signs of the Times*, entitled 'Cain and Abel'. We must not forget, as we indicated at the time, that in constructing the Temple, Solomon had recourse to foreign workers, a particularly significant fact because of the intimate relation which exists between geometry and architecture.

8. Let us recall that the word *gematria* (which, being of Greek origin, must, like a certain number of other terms of the same provenance, have been introduced at a relatively recent period, something that does not mean that what it designates may not have existed earlier), is not derived from *geometria*, as is often claimed, but from *grammateia*, so that once more it is the science of letters that is involved.

9. It is only with Christianity that one can find something like this in Greek, and then it is manifestly a question of a transposition of a symbolism whose origin is Hebraic. In this regard we are alluding principally to the Apocalypse; we could probably also find things of the same order in what remains of Gnostic writings.

too have a numeric value (which is moreover the same as their equivalents in the Hebrew and Arabic alphabets), and since indeed they never had any other numerical signs. The explanation of this fact is nonetheless quite simple. Greek writing is really only a foreign import (whether 'Phoenician', as is usually said, or in any case 'Cadmean', that is to say 'Eastern' without any more precise specification, the very names of the letters bearing witness to this), and never as it were became truly one in its symbolism, numerical or otherwise, with the language itself.[10] On the contrary, in languages such as Hebrew and Arabic, the meaning of the words is inseparable from the symbolism of the letters, and it would be impossible to give a complete interpretation as to the deepest meaning of words, that which really matters from the traditional and initiatic point of view (for we must not forget that these are essentially 'sacred languages'), without taking into account the numerical value of the letters composing them; the relations existing between numerically equivalent words and the substitutions to which they sometimes lend themselves are in this respect a particularly clear example.[11] There is thus something here which, as we said at the outset, relates essentially to the very constitution of these languages, something that belongs to them in a truly 'organic' way and is very far from attaching to it from the outside and after the fact, as in the case of the Greek language; and since this element is found both in Hebrew and Arabic, one can legitimately regard it as proceeding from the

10. Even in the symbolic interpretation of the words (for example in Plato's *Cratylus*), a consideration of the letters of which they are composed does not intervene; it is the same, moreover, for *nirukta* in the Sanskrit language, and if in certain aspects of the Hindu tradition there nonetheless exists a symbolism of letters, even one that is well developed, it is based on principles entirely different from those in question here.

11. This is one of the reasons why the idea, which some extol under the pretext of 'convenience', of writing Arabic with Latin characters is altogether unacceptable, and even absurd (this without prejudice to other more contingent considerations, like the impossibility of establishing a truly exact transcription because of the very fact that all the Arabic letters do not have their equivalent in the Latin alphabet). The real reasons why certain orientalists propagate this idea are moreover quite different from those they profess and must be sought in their 'anti-traditional' designs and in preoccupations of a political order; but that is another story...

common source of these two languages and of the two traditions they express, that is, what can be called the 'Abrahamic' tradition.

From the above considerations we can draw the necessary conclusion, namely that if we look at the science of numbers among the Greeks and among the Hebrews, we see it clothed in two very different forms and based in one case on a geometric symbolism, and in the other on the symbolism of letters.[12] Consequently there can be no question of 'borrowings' on one side any more than on the other, but only of equivalences such as are necessarily to be found among all traditional forms. We leave aside entirely any question of 'priority', which is of no real interest under these conditions, and is perhaps insoluble, for the real starting-point is perhaps very much earlier than the epochs for which it is possible to establish an even slightly rigorous chronology. Moreover, the very hypothesis of a direct common origin must also be ruled out, for the tradition of which this science is an integral part can be seen to date back on the one hand to an 'Apollonian' source, that is to say one that is directly Hyperborean, and on the other to an 'Abrahamic' source, which seems itself to be linked especially (as the very names of the Hebrews and Arabs suggest) to the traditional current that came from the 'lost island of the West'.[13]

12. We say 'based on' because in both cases these symbolisms effectively constitute the sensible 'support' and as it were the 'body' of the science of numbers.

13. We have used the expression 'science of numbers' to avoid any confusion with profane arithmetic, though we could perhaps adopt a term such as 'arithmology'; but because of the 'barbarism' of its hybrid composition we must reject the recently coined term 'numerology', by which some seem to want to designate a sort of 'divinatory art' that has almost no connection with the true traditional science of numbers.

4

LA KABBALE JUIVE
OF PAUL VULLIAUD

UP TO NOW there has existed no serious body of work for the study
of the Kabbalah; indeed, the book by Adolphe Frank, despite his
reputation, showed how its author, imbued as he is with university
prejudices and completely ignorant of Hebrew, was incapable of
understanding the subject he undertook to treat. As for certain
compilations that are as indigestible as they are fanciful, like that
of Papus, better not to speak of them at all. Thus there was a regrettable gap to fill, and it seemed to us that the important work of Paul
Vulliaud[1] was destined precisely for that purpose. However, although this work has been done very conscientiously and contains
many interesting things, we must confess that on reading it we have
felt a certain disappointment.

This work, which we would have been happy to recommend
unreservedly, does not give what its very general title seems to
promise, and the contents of the book are far from being without
defect. Indeed, the subtitle 'Critical Essay' should have put us on
guard as to the spirit in which this book was conceived, for we know
only too well what the word 'critical' means when used by 'official'
scholars; but since Vulliaud does not belong to this category we
were at first merely surprised that he had used an expression susceptible to such an unfortunate interpretation. Later we began to
understand the purpose which the author wished to hint at in this
way; we found it expressed very clearly in a note where he declares

---

1. *La Kabbale juive: histoire et doctrine*, 2 vols., in octavo, of 520 and 460 pages (E.
Nourry: Paris, 1923).

that he had assigned himself a 'double goal': 'To treat of the Kabbalah and its history, then at the same time to explicate the scientific method by which well-respected authors work.' (vol. 2, p206.)

Thus it was not a case of following the authors in question or of adopting their prejudices, but on the contrary of combatting them, for which we can only congratulate him. But he wished to oppose them on their own ground and as it were with their own weapons, and it is for this reason that he became, so to speak, the critic of the critics themselves. Indeed, he too places himself at the point of view of pure and simple erudition; but although he did this voluntarily, one might ask to what extent this attitude has been truly useful and beneficial. Vulliaud denies that he is a Kabbalist; and he does so with an insistence that surprises us and that we find hard to understand. Could he be one of those who glory in being 'profane' and who, up till now, we had for the most part only met in 'official' circles, those toward which he has himself given proof of a just severity? He even goes so far as to qualify himself as a 'simple amateur', but in this we believe he maligns himself. Is he not depriving himself of a good part of the authority he would need when addressing those authors whose assertions he questions? In addition, this bias of looking at a doctrine from the 'profane' point of view, that is, 'from the outside', seems to us to exclude all possibility of a profound comprehension. And furthermore, even if this attitude is only affected, it is no less regrettable since, although he has attained the aforesaid comprehension on his own account, he thus obliges himself to show nothing of it and so the interest of the doctrinal part will be greatly diminished. As for the critical part, the author will look more like a polemicist than a qualified judge, which for him is a manifest inferiority. Besides, two goals for one single work is probably one too many, and in Vulliaud's case it is very regrettable that, as noted above, the second of these goals too often causes him to forget the first, which is however by far the more important. Indeed, discussions and criticisms follow one another right through his book, even in chapters whose titles seem rather to point to a subject of a purely doctrinal order; one comes away with a certain impression of disorder and confusion. On the other hand, if among Vulliaud's criticisms there are some that are perfectly justified, for

example those concerning Renan and Frank and also certain occultists, the latter being the most numerous, there are others that are
more debatable, in particular those concerning Fabre d'Olivet,
toward whom the author seems to direct an echo of certain rabbini-
cal hatreds (unless he inherited the hatred of Napoleon himself for
the author of *Hermeneutic Interpretation of the Origin of the Social
State of Man and of the Destiny of the Adamic Race*, but this second
hypothesis is much less likely).[2] In any case, even for the most legitimate criticisms, those that can be held to destroy usurped reputa-
tions, would it not have been possible to say the same things more
briefly, and especially more seriously and in a less aggressive tone?
The work would certainly have gained by it, first because it would
not have given the appearance of a polemical work, an aspect which
he too often presents and which ill-intentioned people could easily
use against him, and more seriously, the essential would have been
sacrificed less to considerations that are really only secondary and
of rather minor interest. There are still other regrettable faults:
the imperfections of form are sometimes embarrassing; we do not
mean only printing errors, which are quite numerous and of which
the errata only rectify a very small part, but too frequent inaccuracies that are difficult, even with the best of goodwill, to impute to
the typography. Thus, there are various 'slips' which are truly inop-
portune. We have noted a certain number, and, curiously enough,
these are found especially in the second volume, as if it had been
written more hastily. For example, Frank was not a 'professor of
philosophy at Stanislas College' (p 241), but at the Collège de
France, which is something quite different. Also, Vulliaud writes
'Cappelle', and sometimes also 'Capele' for the Hebraist Louis Cap-
pel, whose exact name we can establish with all the more certainty
since, while writing this article, we have his own signature before us.
Would Vulliaud have seen this name only in a latinized form? All
this is nothing much, but, on the other hand, on page 26, it is a
question of a divine name of 26 letters, and we find later that it has
42. This passage is truly incomprehensible and we wonder whether

---

2. For more on Fabre d'Olivet and his works, see *The Great Triad*, chaps. 21 and
22. ED.

there has not been some omission here. We will point out yet another piece of negligence of the same order, but one all the more serious in that it leads to a real injustice: criticizing an editor of the *Encyclopaedia Britannica*, Vulliaud ends with this sentence:

> One could not expect sound logic from an author who in the same article maintains that people have underestimated the Kabbalistic doctrines (*absurdly overestimated*) and at the same time that the Zohar is a *farrago of absurdity* (vol. 2, p 418).

The English words were cited by Vulliaud himself; now, *overestimated* does not mean 'sous-estimé' (which would be *underestimated*), but on the contrary 'surestimé', which is precisely the opposite, and thus, whatever may be the errors contained in that author's article, the contradictions for which he is reproached are in no way found in it. Assuredly, these things are only details, but when one is so severe with others and is ever ready to catch them out, should one not try to be above reproach oneself? In the transcription of Hebrew words there is a lack of uniformity that is truly annoying; we know very well that no transcription can be perfectly exact, but when one has adopted one, whatever it may be, it would be preferable to at least hold to it consistently. Moreover, there are some terms which seem to have been translated much too hastily and for which it would not have been difficult to find a more satisfactory interpretation. For example, on page 49 of volume two, there is an image of *teraphim* on which is inscribed, among others, the word *luz*. The author has reproduced the different meanings of the verb *luz* given by Buxtorf, following each of them with a question mark because it seemed to him to be inappropriate, but he did not think that there might also exist a noun *luz*, which ordinarily means 'almond' or 'kernel' (and also 'almond tree', because it designates the tree and its fruit at the same time). Now, in rabbinic language this same noun is the name of a small indestructible bodily part to which the soul remains bound after death (it is curious to note that this Hebrew tradition probably inspired certain theories of Leibnitz); this last meaning is certainly the most plausible and this is moreover confirmed for us by the very place which the word *luz* occupies in the figure given.

The author sometimes makes the mistake of taking up in passing subjects about which he is obviously much less informed than he is on the Kabbalah, and which he could well have refrained from speaking about, and this would have avoided certain errors which, however excusable they may be (given that it is hardly possible to have the same competence in all fields), can only be prejudicial to a serious work. Thus we found (vol. 2, p377) a passage involving a would-be 'Chinese theosophy' in which we had some trouble recognizing Taoism, which is not 'theosophy' in any sense of the word, the proffered summary of which, made on the basis of we know not what source (no reference being given), is eminently fanciful. For example 'active nature', *T'ien* = heaven, is put in opposition to 'passive nature', *Kouèn* = earth; now *Kouèn* has never meant 'earth', and the expressions 'active nature' and 'passive nature' make us think much less of conceptions from the Far East than of Spinoza's 'nature *naturante*' and *natura naturata*. Two different dualities are here confused with the greatest naïveté, that of 'active perfection', *Khien*, and 'passive perfection', *Kouèn* (we say 'perfection' and not 'nature'), and that of 'heaven', *tièn* and 'earth', *ti*.

Since we have come to speak of Eastern doctrines, we will make another observation on this subject: after noting quite rightly the disagreement that prevails among Egyptologists and among other such 'specialists', and which makes it impossible to trust their opinions, the author points out that the same thing holds true of Indologists (vol. 2, p363), which is correct; but how does he not see that this last case is in no way comparable to the others? Indeed, we obviously have no direct means of verification regarding peoples like the ancient Egyptians and Assyrians, who disappeared without leaving any legitimate successors, and we are certainly right in entertaining some skepticism as to the value of fragmentary and hypothetical reconstitutions. On the contrary, for India and China, whose civilizations have continued down to our own time and are still living, it is quite possible to know what to believe; what matters is not so much what Indologists say but what Hindus themselves think. Vulliaud, who is careful to refer only to Hebrew sources in trying to understand the Kabbalah, is absolutely correct on this point, since the Kabbalah is Hebrew tradition itself, but could he not admit that one should not act otherwise when studying other traditions?

There are other things that Vulliaud does not know much better than he does the doctrines of the Far East, but which ought to have been more accessible to him, if only because of the fact that they are Western. Thus, for example, Rosicrucianism, about which he scarcely seems to know more than the 'profane' and 'official' historians, and whose essentially Hermetic character seems to have escaped him; he only knows that it is something altogether different from the Kabbalah (the occultist and modern idea of a 'Kabbalistic Rosicrucianism' is indeed a pure fantasy), but to support this assertion and not rely on mere negation it would still be necessary to prove precisely that Kabbalah and Hermeticism are two entirely different traditional forms. Still in regard to Rosicrucianism, we do not believe it possible to 'generate a little sympathy for the dignitaries of classical science' by recalling that Descartes tried to contact the Rosicrucians during his stay in Germany (vol. 2, p235), for this fact is quite well known. But what is certain is that he was unsuccessful in his attempt, and that the very spirit of his works, which are as contrary as can be to all esoterism, is both the proof and explanation of this failure. It is surprising to see quoted, as a sign of Descartes' possible affiliation with the Brotherhood of the Rose-Cross, a dedication (that of the *Thesaurus mathematicus*) which is obviously ironic and in which one senses on the contrary all the resentment of a man who was unable to attain the affiliation he sought. Stranger still are Vulliaud's errors concerning Freemasonry. Immediately after making fun of Éliphas Lévi, who did indeed stack confusion upon confusion when he tried to speak of the Kabbalah, Vulliaud also says many no less amusing things when speaking of Freemasonry. We cite the following passage which was meant to establish that there is no link between the Kabbalah and Masonry:

> On the limiting of Masonry to the European frontiers it can be observed that Masonry is universal, worldwide. Is it likewise kabbalistic among the Chinese and the Blacks? (vol. 2, p319).

Certainly the Chinese and African secret societies (of the latter particularly those of the Congo) had no connection with the Kabbalah, but they had no more of a link with Masonry; and if this is not 'limited to the European frontiers' it is only because Europeans have introduced it to other parts of the world. And here is a statement no less curious: 'How does one explain such an anomaly [if it is admitted that Masonry is of Kabbalistic inspiration] as the Freemason Voltaire, who had nothing but scorn for the Jewish race?' Vulliaud seems unaware that Voltaire was received into the lodge 'The Nine Sisters' as a purely honorific gesture, and only six months before his death. On the other hand, even had he chosen a better example, this still would not have proven anything, for there are many Masons, we would even say the greatest number, and even those in the highest grades, to whom all real knowledge of Masonry is completely foreign (and we can include among them certain dignitaries of the *Grand-Orient de France* whom Vulliaud, doubtless letting himself be impressed by their titles, wrongly cites as authorities). Our author would have been better advised to invoke in support of his thesis the fact that in Germany and in Sweden there exist Masonic organizations from which Jews are strictly excluded; we believe that he knew nothing of this for he makes not the slightest allusion to it. It is interesting to extract from the note which ends the same chapter (p328) the following lines:

> Various persons may reproach us for having argued as if there were only one single form of Masonry. We are not unaware of the anathemas of spiritualist Masonry against the *Grand-Orient de France* but when all is duly considered, we feel that the conflict between the two Masonic schools is only a family quarrel.

We will observe that there are not just 'two Masonic schools' but a very great number of them, and that the *Grand-Orient de France*, like that in Italy, is not recognized by the other organizations because it rejects certain *landmarks* or fundamental principles of Masonry, which constitutes, after all, a fairly serious 'quarrel' (whereas among the other 'schools' the divergences are far from being so great). As for the expression 'spiritualist Masonry', it corresponds to absolutely nothing, seeing that it is only an invention of certain occultists whose suggestions he is generally less eager to accept. A little further on he quotes as examples of 'spiritualist

Masonry' the Ku-Klux-Klan and the Orangists (we suppose that this means the Royal Order of Orange), that is, two purely Protestant organizations, which no doubt can count some Masons among their members but which have no more connection with Masonry than the secret societies of the Congo mentioned previously. Assuredly, Vulliaud has every right to be unaware of all these things and many others besides, and we do not think we should reproach him for that; but again, who obliged him to speak of them, given that these questions lie outside his subject and that he could not claim to know absolutely everything about this subject? In any case, if he had stuck to it, he would have had much less trouble gathering, at least on certain of those points, fairly exact information, rather than looking up a number of rare and unknown books that he takes pleasure in quoting with some ostentation.

Of course, all these reservations do not prevent us from recognizing the real merits of the work or from rendering homage to the considerable effort to which it bears witness; quite the contrary, if we have dwelt on his errors so much it is because we think we are rendering a service to an author in criticizing him on very precise points. Now we must say that Vulliaud, in contrast to modern authors who question it (and among them, strange to say, there are many Jews), has done a good job in establishing the antiquity of the Kabbalah as well as its specifically Jewish and strictly orthodox character. Indeed, it is the fashion among 'rationalist' critics to set the esoteric tradition against rabbinic exoterism, as if they were not two complementary aspects of one and the same doctrine. At the same time, he has exploded a certain number of myths that have been broadcast too widely (by those same 'rationalists') and that lack any basis, such as that which tries to link the Kabbalah to Neoplatonic doctrines, that which attributes the Zohar to Moses de Leon (thus making it a work dating only from the thirteenth century), that which claims Spinoza was a Kabbalist, and others of greater or lesser importance. Moreover, he has thoroughly established that the Kabbalah is not at all 'pantheistic' as some have claimed (doubtless because they think it can be linked to the theories of Spinoza which are truly 'pantheistic'); and he very rightly observes that 'this term has been strangely abused' and that it has been used without rhyme or reason for the most varied ideas with the sole intention of 'seeking to frighten' (vol. 1, p429), and also, we might add, because one thus thinks oneself freed from any further discussion. This absurd accusation is gratuitously and very frequently raised against all Eastern doctrines; but it always produces its desired effect on certain timid minds, although by being used abusively the word 'pantheism' ends by no longer meaning anything. When will it be understood that names invented by systems of modern philosophy are applicable to them alone? Vulliaud further shows that a so-called 'mystical philosophy' of the Jews, different from the Kabbalah, is something that has never existed in reality, but on the contrary he is wrong to use the word 'mysticism' to qualify the said Kabbalah. Doubtless that depends on the meaning one gives to this word, and the one he indicates (which would make it almost a synonym of 'Gnosticism' or transcendent knowledge) would be tenable if one did not have to worry about etymology, for it is precisely true that 'mysticism' and 'mystery' have one and the same root (vol. 1, pp124 and 131–132); but in the end it is necessary to take into account the established usage, which has modified and considerably restricted its meaning. On the other hand, it is not possible for us to accept in either one of these two cases the affirmation that 'mysticism is a philosophical system' (p126); and if the Kabbalah too often takes a 'philosophical' appearance in Vulliaud's work, this is a result of the 'outside' point of view he wishes to maintain. For us, the Kabbalah is far more metaphysical than philosophical and more initiatic than mystical; one day we shall have a chance to expound the essential differences that exist between the way of initiates and that of mystics (which, let us note in passing, correspond respectively to the 'dry way' and the 'humid way' of the alchemists).[3] However that may be, the varied results we have noted could henceforth be considered as definitely established if the incomprehension of some so-called scholars did not always come along to put everything in doubt again by going back to a historical point of view to which Vulliaud has accorded (we are tempted to say 'unfortunately', without however failing to recognize its relative importance) too great an importance compared with the

---

3. See *Perspectives on Initiation*, especially chap 1. ED.

properly doctrinal point of view. With regard to the latter, we will note as particularly interesting the chapters in the first volume concerning *En-Soph* and the *Sephiroth* (chap. 60), the *Shekinah* and *Metatron* (chap. 13), although it would have been desirable to find more elaborations and precision there, as well as in the chapter where the Kabbalistic methods are explained (chap. 5). Indeed, we wonder whether those who have no previous knowledge of the Kabbalah would be sufficiently enlightened by reading them.

With regard to what could be called the applications of the Kabbalah, which although secondary with respect to the pure doctrine are certainly not to be neglected, we will mention in the second volume the chapter devoted to ritual (chap. 14) and those devoted to amulets (chap. 15) and to Messianic ideas (chap. 16); these contain things that are really new or at least fairly little known; in particular, one finds in chapter sixteen numerous items of information on the social and political side which contribute in great part to give to the Kabbalistic tradition its clearly and properly Jewish character. Taken as a whole, Vulliaud's work seems to us particularly capable of rectifying a large number of false ideas, which is certainly something, and even a great deal, but perhaps not enough for such an important work and one which wishes to be more than a mere introduction. If the author one day brings out a new edition, it is to be hoped that he will separate the doctrinal part as completely as possible, appreciably curtail the first part, and expand the second, even if in doing so he runs the risk of no longer passing as the 'mere amateur', to which role he has been too keen to confine himself.

To end this discussion of Vulliaud's book we offer a few more observations on a question that particularly merits attention and that has a certain connection with what we have already explained more especially in our study *The King of the World*; we mean that concerning the *Shekinah* and *Metatron*. In its most general sense, the *Shekinah* is the 'real presence' of the Divinity; the first thing we must point out is that the passages of scripture which particularly mention it are especially those concerning the establishment of a spiritual center: the construction of the Tabernacle and the erection of the Temples of Solomon and Zorobabel. Such a center, established in regularly defined conditions, must be the place of divine manifestation, always represented as a 'Light'; and although Vul-liaud denies any connection between the Kabbalah and Masonry (even though he recognizes that the symbol of the 'Great Architect' is a metaphor customary among rabbis), the expression 'a regular and well-illuminated place' which Masonry has preserved really seems to be a memory of the ancient sacerdotal science that pre-sided over the construction of the temples and that moreover is not peculiar to Jews. It is useless for us to tackle here the theory of 'spir-itual influences' (we prefer this expression to 'benedictions' to trans-late the Hebrew *berakoth*, all the more because that is the meaning very clearly preserved in the Arabic word *barakah*); but even consid-ering things from this point of view alone it would be possible to explain the statement of Elias Levita which Vulliaud reports: 'The Masters of the Kabbalah have great secrets on this subject.' Now the question is all the more complex because the *Shekinah* presents itself under multiple aspects. It has two principal aspects, one interior and the other exterior (vol. 1, p 495), but here Vulliaud could have explained himself a little more clearly than he did, all the more so because, in spite of his intention to treat only the 'Jewish Kabbalah', he has pointed out precisely 'the connections between the Jewish and Christian theologies with respect to the *Shekinah*' (p 493). Now in the Christian tradition there is a phrase that very clearly describes the two aspects of which he speaks: *Gloria in excelsis Deo, et in terra Pax hominibus bonae Voluntatis.* The words *Gloria* and *Pax* refer respectively to the inner aspect, with respect to the Principle, and to the outer aspect, with respect to the manifested world; and if one considers these two words in this way one immediately understands why they are pronounced by the Angels (*Malakim*) to announce the birth of 'God with us' or 'in us' (*Emmanuel*). For the first aspect, it would also be possible to recall the theory of the theologians on the 'Light of Glory' in which and by which is accomplished the beatific vision (*in excelsis*). For the second aspect, we will say further that 'Peace' in its esoteric sense is everywhere mentioned as the spiritual attribute of the spiritual centers established in this world (*terra*). On the other hand, the Arabic word *Sakinah*, which is obviously identi-cal with the Hebrew word, is translated by 'Great Peace', the exact equivalent of the *Pax Profunda* of the Rosicrucians; and in this way it would doubtless be possible to explain what they meant by the 'Temple of the Holy Spirit'. One could likewise precisely interpret a certain number of Gospel texts, all the more so as 'the secret tradition concerning the *Shekinah* would have some connection with the light of the Messiah' (p503). Is it thus without meaning it that, in making this last remark, Vulliaud says that it is a question of the tradition 'reserved to those who follow the way which leads to *Pardes*,' that is, as we have explained elsewhere, to the supreme spiritual center? This leads us to observe that when, a little further on, it is a question of a 'mystery relating to the Jubilee' (p506), which is related in a certain sense to the idea of 'Peace', he cites the following text from the *Zohar* (III, p586):

> The river which flows out of Eden bears the name of *Jobel*, like that of Jeremiah (17:8): 'It will extend its roots by the river,' from which it follows that the central idea of the Jubilee is the return of all things to their primitive state.

It is clear that this involves the return to the 'primordial state' envisaged by all traditions and which we dealt with in our study *The Esoterism of Dante*; and when we add from Vulliaud that 'the return of all things to their first state will announce the Messianic era' (p507), those who have read that essay will recall what we said there about the links between the 'Terrestrial Paradise' and the 'Heavenly Jerusalem'.[4] On the other hand, what is involved here, everywhere and always, in the different phases of cyclic manifestation, is the *Pardes*, the center of this world, which the traditional symbolism of all peoples compares to the heart, center of the being and 'divine residence' (*Brahma-pura* in Hindu doctrine), like the tabernacle which is its image and which, for that reason, is called in Hebrew *mishkan* or 'abode of God' (p493), a word with the same root as the word *Shekinah*. From another point of view, the *Shekinah* is the synthesis of the *Sephiroth*; now in the sephirotic tree, the 'right-hand column' is the side of Mercy and the 'left-hand column' is the side of Rigor; we must therefore find these two aspects in the *Shekinah* also. Indeed 'if man sins and withdraws from the *Shekinah*, he falls under

---

4. See *The Esoterism of Dante*, chap 8. ED.

the influence of the powers (*Sārim*) subject to Rigor' (p 507) and then the *Shekinah* is called the 'hand of rigor', which immediately recalls the well-known symbol of the 'hand of justice'. But if on the contrary man draws near to the *Shekinah*, he is freed, and the *Shekinah* is the 'right hand' of God, that is to say that the 'hand of justice' then becomes the 'hand that blesses'. These are the mysteries of the 'House of Justice' (*Beith-Din*), which is yet another name of the supreme spiritual center; and we hardly need point out that the two sides we have considered are those into which the elect and the damned are divided in the Christian representations of the 'Last Judgment'. One could likewise establish a parallel between the two ways which the Pythagoreans represented by the letter 'Y' and which were symbolized exoterically by the myth of Hercules between Virtue and Vice; by the two doors, celestial and infernal, which among the Latins were associated with the symbolism of Janus; and by the two cyclical phases, ascending and descending which among the Hindus were likewise associated with the symbolism of *Ganesha*. Finally, it is easy to understand what is truly meant here when we consider such expressions as 'right intention' and 'goodwill' (*Pax hominibus bonae voluntatis*, and those familiar with the numerous symbols to which we have alluded will see that it is not without reason that Christmas coincides with the winter solstice), when one is careful to leave aside all the outward, philosophical and moral interpretations that have been given them from the Stoics to Kant.

'The Kabbalah gives to the *Shekinah* a 'twin' [*parèdre*], which bears names identical to its own, and which accordingly possesses the same characteristics' (pp 496–498) and which naturally has as many different aspects as the *Shekinah*; its name is *Metatron*, and this name is numerically equal to that of *Shaddaï*, the 'All Powerful' (which is said to be the name of the God of Abraham). The etymology of the word *Metatron* is very uncertain, and Vulliaud reports several hypotheses, one of which derives it from the Chaldean *Mitra* which means 'rain', and which through its root also has a certain connection with 'light'. Even if this is so, the resemblance with the Hindu and Zoroastrian *Mitra* does not constitute a sufficient reason to admit a borrowing by Judaism from foreign doctrines, any more than the role attributed to rain in different Eastern traditions constitutes a borrowing; and on this subject we will point out that Jewish tradition speaks of a 'dew of light' emanating from the 'Tree of Life', by means of which the resurrection of the dead will be accomplished (p 99), and also of an 'effusion of dew' which represents the celestial influence spread to all worlds (p 465), and which curiously recalls the symbolism of the alchemists and Rosicrucians.

'The term *Metatron* includes all such meanings as guardian, Lord, envoy, mediator' (p 499); he is the 'Angel of the Face' and also 'Prince of the World' (*Sār ha-ōlam*); he is the 'author of theophanies, of divine manifestations in the sensible world' (p 492). We will readily admit that he is the 'Celestial Pole'; and since this has its reflection in the 'Terrestrial Pole' with which it is directly related along the 'World Axis', is this not the reason why it is said that *Metatron* himself was Moses' teacher? Let us further cite these lines:

> His name is *Mikaël*, the 'High Priest' who is holocaust and oblation before God. And all that the Israelites do on earth is accomplished in conformity with what happens in the celestial world. The Great Pontiff here below symbolizes *Mikaël*, prince of Clemency.... In all the passages where Scripture speaks of the appearance of *Mikaël*, the glory of the *Shekinah* is involved.' (pp 500–501.)

What is said here of the Israelites can be said of all peoples who possess a truly orthodox tradition; all the more must it be said of the representatives of the primordial tradition, from which all the others derive and to which they are all subordinate. On the other hand, *Metatron* not only has the aspect of Clemency but also that of Justice; in the celestial world he is not only the 'High Priest' (*Kohen ha-gadol*) but also the 'High Prince' (*Sār ha-gadol*), which amounts to saying that in him is found the principle of royal power as well as that of the sacerdotal or pontifical power to which the function of 'mediator' properly corresponds. It should also be noted that *Melek*, 'king', and *Maleak*, 'angel' or 'messenger', are really two forms of the same word; moreover, *Malaki*, 'my messenger' (that is to say, the messenger of God, or 'the angel in which is God', *maleak ha-Elohim*) is the anagram of *Mikaël*. It is fitting to add that although as we have seen *Mikaël* is identified with *Metatron*, he represents only one aspect of him; besides the luminous face there is also a dark face, and we touch here upon other mysteries. Indeed, it may seem strange that Samael is also named *Sār ha-ōlam*, and we are a little surprised that Vulliaud was content to register this fact without the least comment (p512). It is this last aspect, and this one only, that is in an inferior sense 'the guardian spirit of this world', the *Princeps huius mundi* mentioned in the Gospel; and this relationship with *Metatron*, of which he is like the shadow, justifies the use of the same name in a double meaning, and leads one to understand at the same time why the apocalyptic number 666 is also a solar number (it is formed in particular from the name *Sorath*, demon of the Sun, and opposed as such to the angel *Mikaël*). Moreover, Vulliaud remarks that according to Saint Hippolyte, 'the Messiah and the Antichrist both have for an emblem the lion' (vol. 2, p373), which is also a solar symbol; and the same observation could be made for the serpent and for many other symbols. From the Kabbalistic point of view it is again a question of the two opposite faces of *Metatron*; in a more general way one could develop on the basis of this question of the double meaning of symbols an entire theory that does not yet seem to have been clearly expounded. We will not dwell further, at least for the moment, on this side of the question, which is perhaps one of those where one encounters, in trying to explain it, the greatest difficulties.

But let us return to the *Shekinah*: this is represented in the lower world by the last of the ten *Sephiroth*, which is called *Malkuth*, that is to say the 'Kingdom', a designation quite worthy of comment from our point of view (as much as is *Tsedek*, 'the Just', which is sometimes a synonym of it); and *Malkuth* is the 'reservoir into which flow the waters which come from the river on high, that is, all the emanations (graces or spiritual influences) which it pours out in abundance' (vol. 1, p509). This 'river from on high' and the waters that come from it strangely recall the role attributed to the celestial river *Gangā* in the Hindu tradition, and one could also point out that the *Shakti*, of which the *Gangā* is one aspect, does not lack a certain analogy with the *Shekinah*, were it only by reason of the 'providential' function common to them both. We know well that the habitual exclusivism of Judaic ideas is not at ease with such comparisons, but they are none the less real, and for us who are not in the habit of allowing ourselves to be influenced by certain prejudices, they present a very great interest because they are a confirmation of the essential doctrinal unity hidden under the apparent diversity of outward forms.

The reservoir of the celestial waters is naturally identical with the spiritual center of our world, from which well up the four rivers of *Pardes*, making their way to the four cardinal points. For the Hebrews, this spiritual center is the holy Mt Zion, to which they give the name 'heart of the world', and which thus becomes for them the equivalent of the *Meru* of the Hindus or the *Alborj* of the Persians. 'The Tabernacle of the Holiness of Jehovah, the residence of the *Shekinah*, is the Holy of Holies which is the heart of the Temple that is itself the center of Zion (Jerusalem), as Holy Zion is the center of the Land of Israel, and as the land of Israel is the center of the world' (p509).

It is also in this way that Dante presents Jerusalem as the 'spiritual pole', as we have explained elsewhere;[5] but when one departs from the properly Judaic point of view, this representation becomes above all symbolic and no longer constitutes a localization in the strict sense of the word. All secondary spiritual centers, established in view of different adaptations of the primordial tradition to given conditions, are images of the supreme center. Zion may really be only one of the secondary centers, but despite this it can be identified symbolically with the supreme center by virtue of this analogy; and what we have already said regarding the 'Holy Land', which is not only the Land of Israel, will enable us to understand this more easily. Another very remarkable expression, as a synonym of 'Holy Land', is 'Land of the Living'; it is said that 'the Land of the Living comprises seven lands', and Vulliaud remarks in this connection that 'this land is Canaan, in which there were seven peoples' (vol. 2. p116).

Doubtless this is correct in the literal sense; but would not these seven lands correspond symbolically to the seven *Dvīpas* which,

5. See *The Esoterism of Dante*, chap 8. ED.

according to the Hindu tradition, have *Meru* as their common center? And if this is so, when the ancient worlds or the creations anterior to ours are represented by the 'seven kings of Edom' (the number is related to the seven 'days' of Genesis), is there not a resemblance, too strongly emphasized to be accidental, to the ages of the seven *Manus* that have elapsed from the beginning of the *Kalpa* up to the present time? We present these few thoughts only as an example of conclusions it is possible to draw from the information contained in Vulliaud's work; unfortunately, it is much to be feared that most readers may not be able to perceive this and draw conclusions from it on their own. But by following up our critique with more doctrinal considerations, we have done a little, within the limits we necessarily had to set ourselves, of what we would have hoped to find in Vulliaud himself.

5

THE *SIPHRA*
DI-TZENIUTHA

As THE FIRST OF A SERIES of 'fundamental texts of the Kabbalah',
Paul Vulliaud has just published a translation of the *Siphra di-Tzeniutha*,[1] preceded by a long introduction, much longer than the
translation itself, or rather the two translations, for there are two
successive versions of the text in this volume, one literal and the
other paraphrased. This introduction seems intended especially to
demonstrate that such a work is far from being useless, even after
the *Zohar* of Jean de Pauly; thus, the greater part of it is devoted to a
detailed account of the said French translation, an account contain-
ing, it seems, almost everything it is possible to know about the
translator himself, a truly enigmatic personage whose origins are
not yet fully clarified. This whole story is very curious, and it is not
beside the point, in order to explain the gaps and the imperfections
of this work, to know under what conditions it was realized and
what strange difficulties the editor had with the unfortunate Jean de
Pauly, who was afflicted by a persecution mania. Nevertheless, we
feel that such details have been given too great a place; on reading
them, one begins to regret that Vulliaud did not devote himself
entirely to what can be called the lesser details of the story, for he
surely would have brought to them an unusual zest; but the Kabbalistic studies would have lost a great deal had he done so.

Concerning the present state of these studies, this same introduction contains general considerations in the course of which Vulliaud
attacks, as only he knows how, the 'Doctors', that is, the 'officials'

1. See *The King of the World*, chap. 10, n4. ED.

about whom he had already spoken some harsh truths in his *Kab-bale juive*, and then a Jesuit priest, Fr. Bonsirven, whom some it seems are now trying to present as an incomparable authority on the subject of Judaism. This discussion is the occasion for some very interesting remarks, especially on the methods of the Kabbalists and on the manner—adjudged 'astounding' by the critics—in which they cite scriptural texts; in this connection Vulliaud adds:

> Contemporary exegesis has shown itself particularly incapable of adequately analyzing Gospel 'quotations' because it is determined to ignore the procedures of Jewish hermeneutics; one must take oneself to Palestine, since the evangelical works were elaborated in this region.

This seems to accord, at least in tendency, with the works of another Jesuit Father, Marcel Jousse, and it is a pity that he is not mentioned, for it would have been interesting to have him thus confront his colleague... On the other hand, Vulliaud very properly points out that Catholics who scoff at the magic formulas, or what are called such, contained in Kabbalistic works, and who hasten to label them as superstitious, ought really to notice that their own rituals are filled with things of the same kind. Likewise for the accusation of 'eroticism' and 'obscenity' brought against a certain type of symbolism:

> Catholic critics might reflect, before adding their voices to those of rationalist Jews and Protestants, that Catholic theology is susceptible, like the Kabbalah, of easily becoming an object of derision regarding what occupies us at present.

It is good that these things are said by a writer who himself professes Catholicism, and certain fanatical anti-Semites and anti-Masons ought to take profit from this excellent lesson.

There are also many other things to point out in the introduction, notably regarding the Christian interpretation of the *Zohar*. Vulliaud makes some apt qualifications regarding certain rather forced comparisons made by Drach and accepted by Jean de Pauly. He also returns to the question of the antiquity of the *Zohar*, which the adversaries of the Kabbalah are bent on challenging for very poor reasons. But there is something else that is a pleasure to point out: Vulliaud states that 'to properly translate certain essential passages, it is necessary to be initiated into the mysteries of Jewish esoterism,' and that 'de Pauly undertook the translation of the *Zohar* without having this initiation'; further on he notes that the Gospel of St John, as well as the Apocalypse, was 'addressed to initiates,' and we could find still other similar statements. There is thus a certain change of attitude with Vulliaud for which we can only congratulate him, for until now he seemed to have a strange reluctance to utter the word 'initiation', or at least if he did, it was really only to mock certain 'initiates' whom he ought rather, to avoid all regrettable confusion, to have qualified as pseudo-initiates. What he writes now is the exact truth; it is indeed 'initiation' in the proper sense of the word that is in question, both in the Kabbalah and in every other esoterism worthy of the name; and we must add that this goes much further than the deciphering of a sort of cryptography, which is what Vulliaud seems to have especially in mind when he speaks as we have just seen. Doubtless this too exists; but this is still only a question of outward form, though the outward form is far from being negligible since one must pass through it to arrive at an understanding of the doctrine. But one must not confuse the means with an end nor place them on the same plane.

However that may be, it is quite certain that most often the Kabbalists may really be speaking of something very different from what they appear to be speaking of, and this is not peculiar to them, far from it, for one finds it also in the Western Middle Ages. We had occasion to examine this subject in connection with Dante and the 'Fedeli d'Amore', and we noted then the principal reasons for it, which do not all reduce to mere prudence as the 'profane' may be tempted to suppose.[2] The same thing also exists in Islamic esoterism, developed to a point that no one, we believe, could suspect in the Western world; moreover, the Arabic language as well as the Hebrew language lends itself to this admirably. Here we find not only the usual symbolism, which Luigi Valli has shown in the work we spoke of to be common to both Sufis and the 'Fedeli d'Amore', but much that is better still. Is it conceivable to Western minds that

2. See *Insights into Christian Esoterism*, chaps. 4 and 5. ED.

a mere treatise on grammar or geography, or even on commerce, should at the same time possess another meaning that makes it an initiatic work of great importance? So it is nonetheless, and these are not chance examples; these three cases are from books that very really exist and that we actually have in our hands.

This leads us to express a slight criticism concerning Vulliaud's translation of the title *Siphra di-Tzeniutha*. He writes 'Secret Book', and not 'Book of the Secret', and the reasons he gives seem rather inconclusive. It is indeed puerile to imagine, as some have done, that 'this title recalls the flight of Simeon ben Yohaï, during which time that rabbi is said to have composed this opuscule in secret'; but this is hardly what is meant by 'Book of the Secret', which really has a much higher and deeper meaning than that of 'Secret Book'. Here we allude to the important role played in certain initiatic traditions, precisely those which interest us now, by the idea of a 'secret' (in Hebrew *sod*, in Arabic *sirr*), which has nothing to do with discretion or dissimulation but is thus by the very nature of things;[3] must we recall in this connection that the Christian Church itself in its first days had a 'discipline of the secret', and that the word 'mystery' in its original sense properly designates the inexpressible?

As for the translation itself, we said there were two versions, and they are not redundant, for the literal version, useful as it may be for those who wish to go back to the text and follow it closely, is often unintelligible. It is always like this, as we have said many times, in the case of sacred books or other traditional writings, and if a translation had to be 'word for word' in the scholarly and academic fashion, one would have to declare them really untranslatable. In reality, for us who place ourselves at a completely different point of view from that of the linguists, it is in truth the paraphrased and annotated version that constitutes the meaning of the text and allows it to be understood, while the literal version sometimes has the effect of a sort of 'word-puzzle', as Vulliaud says, or an incoherent rambling. We only regret that the commentary is not more extensive and explicit; the notes, although numerous and very interesting, are not always sufficiently 'illuminating', so to speak, and it is to be feared

3. See *Perspectives on Initiation*, chap. 13. Ed.

that they may not be understood by those who do not already have a more than elementary knowledge of the Kabbalah; but doubtless we must await the sequel of these 'fundamental texts', which, it is to be hoped, will felicitously complete this first volume. Vulliaud owes it both to us and himself to provide a similar work on the *Iddra Rabba* and *Iddra Zuta* which, with the *Siphra di-Tzeniutha*, are as he says far from being simply annexes or appendices of the *Zohar*, but 'are on the contrary its central parts', those which contain as it were in the most concentrated form all the essential part of the doctrine.

REVIEWS

Le Scorpion, symbole du peuple juif dans l'art religieux des XIVe, XVe, XVIe siècles, by MARCEL BULARD (Paris: Éditions de Boccard, 1935). Starting with an examination of paintings in the Chapel of St Sebastian de Lans-le-Villard in Savoy, the author has collected all the relevant documents he was able to discover and has made a very detailed study of them, accompanied by many reproductions. Under discussion are representations of the scorpion, either on the standard carried by the personified Synagogue, or more frequently in the representations of certain scenes of the Passion. In this last case, the scorpionic standard is generally associated with standards bearing other emblems, and especially the letters S P Q R, obviously to indicate the participation of both the Jews and the Romans. A rather curious thing that seems to have escaped the author's attention is that these same letters, arranged in another order (S Q R P), evoke phonetically the very name of the scorpion. As for the interpretation of this symbol, the author, basing himself on the 'Bestiaries' as well as on the dramatic poetry of the end of the Middle Ages, shows that it especially signifies falsity and perfidy; he quite rightly remarks, moreover, that during the period in question symbolism, far from being 'dogmatic' as it was previously, became principally 'moral', which amounts to saying that it was on the verge of degenerating into mere 'allegory', a direct consequence of the weakening of the traditional spirit. Be that as it may, we think that, originally at least, there must have been something more, perhaps an allusion to the zodiacal sign of Scorpio, to which the idea of death is attached; besides, we may note in this regard that without such an allusion the very passage of the Gospel where the scorpion is opposed to the egg (Luke 11:11–12) remains per-fectly incomprehensible. Another interesting and enigmatic point is the attribution of the same symbols, in particular the scorpion and the basilisk, to the Synagogue and to Dialectic. Here the explanations considered, such as the reputation for dialectical skill that the Jews had, seem to us truly insufficient to explain such an association; and we cannot help but recall a tradition according to which the works of Aristotle, who was considered the master of Dialectic, must have con-tained a hidden meaning that cannot be penetrated and applied except by the Antichrist, who on the other hand, it is said, must be of Jewish descent. Is there not something to look for in this direction?

Sir Charles Marston, *La Bible a dit vrai*, tr. Luce Clarence (Paris: Librairie Plon, 1935) [orig. English, *The Bible is True: the Lessons of the 1925–1934 Excavation in Bible Lands Summarized and Explained* (London: The Religious Book Club, 1934)]. First and foremost this book contains, if one may put it so, an excellent criticism of biblical 'criticism', bringing out perfectly all that is partial in its methods and mistaken in its conclusions. Moreover, it seems that the position of this 'criticism', formerly so self-assured, is today seriously compro-mised in the eyes of many, for all the recent archeological discoveries only bring more refutations. Perhaps this is the first time that such discoveries serve for something that goes beyond mere erudition... It goes without saying moreover that those who truly know what tradi-tion is have never had any need for this kind of proof; but it must be recognized that, being based on facts that are as it were 'material' and tangible, they are especially fitted to appeal to the modern spirit, which is sensitive only to things of this order. We will note in particu-lar that the results obtained go directly against all the 'evolutionist' theories, and that they show 'monotheism' at the very origins and not as the final outcome of a long development starting from a so-called primitive 'animism'. Another interesting point is the proof of the existence of alphabetic writing at the time of Moses, and even earlier; and texts almost contemporaneous with him describe rites similar to those of the Pentateuch, which the 'critics' claimed to be of late insti-tution. Finally, numerous historical facts reported in the Bible, the authenticity of which was challenged, are now found to be entirely confirmed. Of course, there still remain besides this many more or less doubtful points; and what we must be wary of is not to go too far in the direction of a narrow and exclusive 'literalism', which, whatever one might say, has absolutely nothing traditional about it in the true sense of the word. It is questionable whether one may speak of a 'biblical chronology' when one goes back beyond Moses. The epoch of Abraham might well be more remote than is supposed. And as for the Deluge, the date that some assign to it would oblige us to reduce its importance to that of a local and very secondary catastrophe, comparable to the floods of Deucalion and Ogyges. As to the origins of humanity, it is necessary to be wary of the obsession with the Caucasus and Mesopotamia, which also has nothing traditional about it and arose solely from interpretations formulated when certain things were no longer understood in their true sense. We can hardly dwell here on certain more particular points, but let us nonetheless note this: how, while recognizing that 'Melchizedek was regarded as a very mysterious personage' in every tradition, can one bring oneself to make him merely the king of some small city, which moreover was not called Salem, but Jebus? And furthermore, if one wishes to place the country of Midian beyond the Gulf of Akaba, what does one do with the tradition that the location of the Burning Bush is to be found in the crypt of the monastery of Saint Catherine, at the very foot of Sinai? But of course, all this in no way diminishes the value of the really important discoveries, which will doubtless continue to multiply, all the more, since, after all, their first appearance goes back only some ten years; and we can only recommend the reading of this clear and conscientious account to all who wish to find arguments against this destructive and anti-traditional 'criticism'. But we are obliged to end with a 'warning' against another point of view: the author seems to rely on modern 'metapsychics' to explain miracles or at least to have them accepted, along with the gift of prophecy and in general links with what he rather unfortunately calls the 'Invisible' (a word which occultists of every category have used and abused all too much); moreover, he is not alone in this, and we have become aware recently of other examples of a similar tendency. This is a regrettable illusion, and there is even, from this perspective, a danger that is all the greater as one is less aware of it. It must not be forgotten that 'diabolical ruses' take all forms, according to circumstances, and attest to almost inexhaustible resources!

PART IV

1

THE HERMETIC
TRADITION

UNDER THE TITLE *La Tradizione Ermetica nei suoi Simboli, nella sua Dottrina e nella sua 'Ars Regia',*[1] Julius Evola has recently published a work that is interesting in many respects, but which just once more illustrates, as if this were needed, the timeliness of what we wrote recently on the relationships between priestly initiation and royal initiation.[2] We find affirmed here the independence of the second, to which the author wishes precisely to link Hermeticism, and the idea of two distinct and even irreducible traditional types, one contemplative and the other active, which generally characterize of the East and the West respectively. Thus we make certain reservations about the interpretation given of Hermetic symbolism, in the measure that it is influenced by such a conception, although elsewhere it clearly shows that true alchemy is of the spiritual and not the material order, which is the exact truth, a truth too often misunderstood or ignored by modern writers who claim to deal with these questions.

We will take advantage of this occasion to further clarify some important ideas, first of all the meaning which should be attributed to the word 'Hermeticism' itself, which some of our contemporaries

---

1. G. Laterza: Bari, 1931. This work has since appeared in a French translation. [See the recent English translation, *The Hermetic Tradition: Symbols & Teachings of the Royal Art* (Inner Traditions International: Rochester, VT, 1995). ED.]

2. Cf. *Perspectives on Initiation*, chap. 40. [Cf. also *Spiritual Authority and Temporal Power.* ED.]

seem to use without rhyme or reason. This word indicates that we
are dealing essentially with a tradition of Egyptian origin, later
cloaked in a Hellenized form, doubtless in the Alexandrian epoch,
and transmitted in this form during the Middle Ages to both the
Islamic and the Christian worlds, and, let us add, to the second
largely by the intermediary of the first, as is proven by the numerous Arabic or arabicized terms adopted by the European Hermeticists, beginning with the word 'alchemy' (*al-Kimia*) itself.[3] It would
therefore be quite illegitimate to extend this designation to other
traditional forms, just as it would be, for example, to call 'Kabbalah'
anything other than Hebrew esoterism; not, of course, that there
exist no equivalents elsewhere, for these exist to the point that this
traditional science of alchemy has its exact correspondence in doctrines such as those of India, Tibet, and China, although with
modes of expression and methods of realization that are naturally
quite different. But as soon as one says 'Hermeticism', one specifies a
clearly determined form, whose provenance can only be Greco-
Egyptian. Indeed, the doctrine thus designated is by this very fact
related to *Hermes* insofar as he was considered by the Greeks to be
identical with the Egyptian *Thoth*; and we will note immediately
that this goes against Evola's thesis by presenting this doctrine as
derived essentially from a sacerdotal teaching, for *Thoth*, in his role
as preserver and transmitter of tradition, is nothing other than the
very representation of the ancient Egyptian priesthood, or rather, to
speak more exactly, of the principle of inspiration from which it
held its authority and in whose name it formulated and communi-
cated initiatic knowledge.

Now a question must be asked: does what has been preserved
under the name of 'Hermeticism' constitute a complete traditional
doctrine? The answer can only be negative, for strictly speaking the
knowledge it represents is not metaphysical but only cosmological
(understanding this in its double application, 'macrocosmic' and
'microcosmic'). It is therefore not admissible that Hermeticism, in
the sense that this word has acquired since the Alexandrian period

3. This word is Arabic in its form but not in its root. It probably derives from the
name *Kemi* or 'Black Earth' given to ancient Egypt.

and held constantly since then, represents the whole of the Egyptian tradition. Although the cosmological point of view seems to have been particularly developed here, and is in any case what is most apparent in all the vestiges that remain, whether it be texts or monuments, it must not be forgotten that it can never be anything but a secondary and contingent point of view, an application of the doctrine to the knowledge of what we can call the 'intermediary world'. It would be interesting, though no doubt rather difficult, to examine how this part of the Egyptian tradition could have found itself as it were isolated and yet remain apparently independent, and then be incorporated into the Islamic and Christian esoterisms of the Middle Ages (which a complete doctrine could not have achieved), to the point of truly becoming an integral part of both and furnishing them with an entire symbolism which, through a suitable transposition, could even serve on occasion as a vehicle for truths of a higher order. This is not the place to enter into these very complex historical considerations, but however that may be, we must say that, even if the specifically cosmological character of Hermeticism does not justify Evola's conception, it at least explains it in a certain measure, for sciences of this order are those which, in all traditional civilizations, have been pre-eminently the appanage of the Kshatriyas or their equivalents, whereas pure metaphysics was that of the Brahmins. This is why one sometimes witnesses as an effect of the revolt of the Kshatriyas against the spiritual authority of the Brahmins the formation of incomplete traditional currents, reduced to these single sciences separated from their principle, and even deviated in a 'naturalist' direction by a negation of metaphysics and the misunderstanding of the subordinate character of 'physical' science and (the two things being closely connected) the sacerdotal origin of all initiatic teaching, even that more particularly intended for the use of the Kshatriyas, as we have explained on other occasions.[4] This is certainly not to say that Hermeticism in itself constitutes such a deviation or that it essentially implies something illegitimate (which would have made its incorporation into traditional orthodox forms impossible); but it is quite necessary to recognize that it

4. See in particular *Spiritual Authority and Temporal Power.*

can easily lend itself to this by its very nature, and this more generally is the danger of all traditional sciences when they are cultivated
for themselves alone, something that exposes them to the danger of
losing sight of their attachment to the principial order. Alchemy,
which could be defined as the 'technique' of Hermeticism, is truly a
'royal art', if this is understood to be a mode of initiation particularly appropriate to the nature of Kshatriyas; but this itself marks its
exact place in the ensemble of a regularly constituted tradition, and
one must furthermore not confuse the means to initiatic realization
with its final goal, which is always pure knowledge.

Another point in Evola's thesis that seems questionable is the
assimilation he almost always makes between Hermeticism and
magic, It is true that he seems to take 'magic' in a rather different
sense from what is ordinarily understood, but we greatly fear that
even this cannot but occasion some rather unfortunate confusions.
Inevitably, when one thinks of 'magic', one thinks of a science meant
to produce more or less extraordinary phenomena, notably (but not
exclusively) in the sensible order. Whatever the origin of the word
may have been, this meaning has become so thoroughly inherent in
it that it ought to be left as it is. Thus it is nothing but the most inferior of the applications of traditional knowledge, we could even say
the most despised, whose practice is left to those whose individual
limitations make them incapable of developing other possibilities;
we see no benefit to evoking the idea when it is really a question
of things that, even though contingent, are nonetheless notably
higher, and even if this is only a question of terminology it must be
agreed that it still has its importance. Besides, something more may
be involved here; this word 'magic' exercises a strange fascination on
some people in our time, and as we have already noted in the
preceding article to which we alluded in the beginning, the prepon-
derance accorded to such a point of view, be this only in intention, is
still linked to the alteration of traditional sciences separated from
their metaphysical principle; and this is doubtless the rock which
every attempt at reconstituting such sciences strikes against, if one
does not begin from what is truly the beginning in all respects, that
is to say with the principle itself, which is also the end in view of
which all the rest must normally be ordered.

On the other hand, where we are entirely in agreement with Evola, and where we see the greatest merit of his book, is when he insists on the purely spiritual and 'interior' nature of true alchemy, which has absolutely nothing to do with the material operations of any 'chemistry' in the natural meaning of this word. Nearly all the moderns are strangely mistaken about this, both those who would make themselves defenders of alchemy as well as those who have made themselves its detractors. It is nevertheless easy to see in what terms the ancient Hermeticists speak of the 'puffers' and 'charcoal burners', in whom must be recognized the true precursors of present-day chemists, unflattering as this may be for them; even as late as the eighteenth century an alchemist like Pernéty does not fail to stress the difference between 'Hermetic philosophy' and 'common chemistry'. Thus, what gave birth to modern chemistry is not alchemy, with which it has in the final analysis no relationship (any more than does the 'hyperchemistry' dreamed up by some contemporary occultists); it is only a deformation or deviation resulting from the incomprehension of those who, incapable of penetrating the true meaning of the symbols, took everything literally and, believing that only material operations were involved, embarked on a program of more or less disordered experimentation. In the Arab world too, material alchemy has always been held of little worth, sometimes even likened to a kind of sorcery, whereas spiritual alchemy, the only true alchemy, was held in high honor, being often designated by the name *Kimia-es-saādah* or 'alchemy of felicity'.[5]

This is not to say, however, that one must deny for this reason the possibility of the metallic transmutations that represent alchemy in the eyes of the common man; but we must not confuse things of wholly different orders, and we do not even see *a priori* why such transmutations could not be achieved through procedures belonging merely to profane chemistry (the 'hyperchemistry' to which we alluded earlier really amounts to no more than this). There is, however, another aspect to the question which Evola very correctly points out. Anyone who has realized certain inner states can, by virtue of the analogical relationship between the 'microcosm' and the

---

5. There exists a treatise of Al-Ghazzali bearing this title.

'macrocosm', produce outwardly corresponding effects. It is therefore admissible that the one who has reached a certain degree in the practice of spiritual alchemy may be thereby capable of accomplishing metallic transmutations, but this only as a wholly accidental consequence and without recourse to any of the procedures of material pseudo-alchemy, solely by a kind of outward projection of the energies he carries within himself. There is a difference here comparable to that separating 'theurgy', or the action of 'spiritual influences', from magic and even sorcery; if the apparent effects are sometimes the same in both cases, the causes which bring them about are totally different. We will add moreover that those who really possess such powers generally make no use of them, at least outside of very particular circumstances where their exercise is made lawful by other considerations. Be that as it may, what must never be lost sight of, and what lies at the very foundation of all truly traditional teaching, is that every realization worthy of the name is of an essentially inward order, even if it is susceptible of outward repercussions. Man can find its principles and means only within himself, and he can do so because he carries within himself a correspondence with all that exists. *Al-insānu ramzul-wujūd*, 'man is a symbol of universal Existence'; and if he succeeds in penetrating to the center of his own being, he thereby attains total knowledge with all that it implies in addition. *Man yaraf nafsahu yaraf Rabbahu*, 'he who knows his self knows his Lord'; and he then knows all things within the supreme unity of the Principle itself, outside of which there is nothing that can have the slightest degree of reality.

2

HERMES

WHEN SPEAKING EARLIER about the Hermetic tradition we said that this properly refers to a knowledge that is not metaphysical but only cosmological, understanding this last in both its 'macrocosmic' and 'microcosmic' senses. Although this was only the expression of the strict truth, it was unfortunately enough to displease some who, viewing Hermeticism through their own fantasies, would like it to contain any and everything. It is true that such people hardly know what pure metaphysics is. However this may be, it must be understood that by saying that we in no way wished to depreciate the traditional sciences that belong to Hermeticism nor those that correspond to them in the other doctrinal forms of the East or West; but one has to know how to put each thing in its place, and these sciences, like any specialized knowledge, remain secondary and derivative with respect to principles, of which they are only the application to a lower level of reality. Only those who would give the 'Royal Art' preeminence over the 'Sacerdotal Art' can claim the contrary;[1] and perhaps this is at root the more or less conscious reason for the protestations just alluded to.

Without otherwise concerning ourselves with what anyone else may think or say, for we are not accustomed to taking into account such individual opinions which, for tradition, do not exist, it seems

---

1. We have considered this question in *Spiritual Authority and Temporal Power*. With regard to the expression 'Royal Art', which Freemasonry still uses, we may note here the curious resemblance between the names *Hermes* and *Hiram*; needless to say, this does not mean that these two names share a common linguistic origin, but their composition is nonetheless identical, and the combination HRM, from which both are essentially formed, also suggests other comparisons.

that it might not be useless to add some new details confirming what we have already said, by focusing more particularly on Hermes, for at least no one contests that it is from Hermes that Hermeticism takes its name.[2] The Greek Hermes has in fact characteristics that correspond exactly to the sciences in question and that are especially expressed by his chief emblem, the caduceus, the symbolism of which we will no doubt find some other occasion to examine more fully. Suffice it to say for the moment that this symbolism relates essentially and directly to what might be called 'human alchemy'[3] that concerns possibilities of the subtle state, even if these are taken merely as the preparatory means to a higher realization, as the equivalent *Hatha-Yoga* practices are in the Hindu tradition. This can, moreover, be transferred to the cosmic order, since everything in man has its correspondence in the world, and inversely;[4] here again, and by reason of this very correspondence, the domain in question is the 'intermediary world', where forces are brought into play whose dual nature is very clearly figured by the two serpents of the caduceus. We will also recall in this connection that Hermes is represented as the messenger of the gods and as their

2. We must emphasize that Hermeticism is really of Helleno-Egyptian provenance, and that one cannot without abuse extend this term to what under diverse forms corresponds to it in other traditions, any more than one can, for example, call 'Kabbalah' a doctrine that is not specifically Hebraic. No doubt, if we were writing in Hebrew, we would use *qabbalah* to designate the tradition in general, just as, writing in Arabic, we would call initiation under any form *taṣawwuf*; but transposed into another language the words in Hebrew, Arabic, etc., must be reserved for the traditional forms of which their languages of origin are the respective expression, whatever may otherwise be the comparisons or even the assimilations to which they may legitimately give rise; and one must not in any case confuse a certain order of knowledge, envisaged in itself, with some special form it may have taken on in particular historical circumstances.

3. See *Man and His Becoming according to the Vedānta*, chap. 21.

4. As is said in the *Rasā'il Ikhwān as-Safā*, 'The world is a great man and man is a little world' (*al-ālam insān kabir wa'l-insān ālam seghir*). It is moreover by virtue of this correspondence that a certain realization in the 'microcosmic' order can bring about, as an accidental consequence for the being that has achieved it, an outward realization relating to the 'macrocosmic' order without it having been especially sought for itself, as we remarked in certain cases of metallic transmutation in the preceding chapter, 'The Hermetic Tradition'.

interpreter (*hermeneutes*), that is, precisely, as an intermediary between the celestial and terrestrial worlds, and that he has in addition the function of a 'psychopomp' [guide of the souls of the dead] which, in a lower order, is clearly related to the domain of subtle possibilities.[5]

It might be objected that in Hermeticism, Hermes takes the place of the Egyptian Thoth, with whom he was identified, and that Thoth properly represents Wisdom, which relates to the priesthood as the guardian and transmitter of the tradition. That is true enough, but since this assimilation cannot have been made without some reason, it must be admitted that it is more particularly a certain aspect of Thoth that is considered here, one corresponding to a certain part of the tradition that includes the branches of knowledge relating to the intermediary world; and in fact, all that can be known of the ancient Egyptian civilization from its vestiges shows precisely that this kind of knowledge was much more developed there and had acquired more importance there than anywhere else. There is besides another comparison, we might even say another equivalence, which shows clearly that this objection has no real significance: in India, the planet Mercury (or Hermes) is called *Budha*, a name whose root means Wisdom; here again, it is enough to determine the order where this Wisdom, which in its essence is the inspiring principle of all knowledge, is to find its more particular application when it is related to this specialized function.[6]

As concerns the name *Budha*, it is curious to note that it is in fact identical to the Scandinavian *Odin*, *Woden*, or *Wotan*;[7] it is thus not

5. Astrologically, the two functions of messenger of the gods and psychopomp can be respectively related to a diurnal and nocturnal aspect; on the other hand, the same correspondence can be found in them as between the ascending and descending currents symbolized by the two serpents of the caduceus.

6. The name *Budha* must not be confused with *Buddha*, the name of Shākya-muni, although both obviously have the same root meaning; moreover, certain aspects of the planetary *Budha* were later transferred to the historical *Buddha*, who is represented as having been 'illuminated' by the irradiation of this star, whose essence he is said to have absorbed. Let us note here that the mother of the Buddha is called *Māyā-Devī* and that, for the Greeks and Romans, *Maïa* was also the mother of Hermes or Mercury.

7. The change of *b* to *v* or *w* is a very common linguistic phenomenon.

at all arbitrary that the Romans assimilated Odin to Mercury, and in some Germanic languages the day of Mercury (in French *mercredi*) is still called the day of Odin.[8] What is perhaps even more remarkable is that this same name is found in the *Votan* of the ancient traditions of Central America, who moreover has the attributes of Hermes, for he is *Quetzalcoatl*, the 'bird-serpent', and the union of these two symbolic animals (corresponding respectively to air and fire) is also figured by the wings and the serpents of the caduceus.[9] One must indeed be blind not to see in such facts a sign of the fundamental unity of all traditional doctrines; unfortunately, such blindness is only too common in our time, where those who truly know how to read symbols are now a tiny minority, and where we find on the contrary all too many 'profane ones' who think themselves qualified to interpret 'sacred science', which they fit to the measure of their own more or less confused imagination.

Another no less interesting point is that in the Islamic tradition the prophet Idrīs is identified both with Hermes and with Enoch; this double assimilation seems to indicate a continuity of tradition going back before the Egyptian priesthood, for this latter merely inherited what Enoch represented, and he manifestly relates to an earlier period.[10] At the same time, the sciences attributed to Idrīs

---

8. 'Wednesday' has exactly the same connotation in English. ED.

9. On this subject see 'The Language of the Birds' (*Symbols of Sacred Science,* chap. 7), where we pointed out that the serpent is opposed or associated with the bird according to whether it is envisaged in its malefic or benefic aspect. We will add that a figure like that of an eagle holding a serpent in its talons (which is to be found precisely in Mexico) does not evoke exclusively the idea of the antagonism represented in the Hindu tradition by the combat of *Garuda* against the *Nāga*. On occasion, especially in heraldic symbolism, the serpent is replaced by a sword (a substitution that is all the more striking when the weapon in question has the form of a flaming sword, which can be linked to the lightning in the clutch of Jupiter's eagle), and the sword, in its highest signification, represents Wisdom and the power of the Word (see, for example, Rev. 1:16). — It may be noted that one of the chief symbols of the Egyptian Thoth was the ibis, destroyer of reptiles, which on this basis became a symbol of Christ; but in the caduceus of Hermes we have the serpent in its two contrary aspects, as in the figure of the medieval 'amphisbaena' (see *The King of the World*, chap. 3, n20).

10. Should it not be concluded from this assimilation that the *Book of Enoch*, or at any rate what is known by this name, must be considered to be an integral part of

and placed under his special influence are not the purely spiritual sciences, which are attributed to the prophet Aissa, that is, to Christ, but the sciences that can be qualified as 'intermediary', among which alchemy and astrology belong in the first rank; these are indeed the sciences that can properly be called Hermetic. But this brings us to another consideration, which, at least at first glance, might seem to indicate a rather strange reversal of the usual correspondences. Among the principal prophets, a particular one, as we shall see in a future study, presides over each of the planetary heavens and is its 'Pole' (al-Quṭb). Now, it is not Idrīs who presides over the heaven of Mercury, but Aissa [Jesus], whereas Idrīs presides over the heaven of the sun; and this naturally involves the same transposition in the astrological correspondences of the sciences that are respectively attributed to them. This raises a very complex question which we could not hope to treat fully here; perhaps we shall have occasion to come back to it, but for the moment we will confine ourselves to a few remarks which will perhaps enable us to glimpse the solution, and will in any case at least show that there is something altogether different here from a simple confusion, and which what might pass for such in the eyes of a superficial and 'outward' observer is in reality based on very profound notions.

First, this is not an isolated case among all the traditional doctrines, for one can find something similar in Hebrew angelology. Generally, *Mikaël* is the angel of the sun, and Raphael is the angel of Mercury, but it sometimes happens that these roles are reversed. On the other hand, if *Mikaël*, insofar as he represents the solar *Metatron*, is esoterically assimilated to Christ,[11] Raphael, according to the meaning of his name, is the 'divine healer', while Christ also appears as 'spiritual healer' and as 'restorer'; one could find also other connections between Christ and the principle represented by Mercury

---

the whole corpus of 'Hermetic books'? On the other hand, some also say that the prophet Idrīs is the same as the Buddha. What has already been said shows well enough how we are to understand this assertion, which really refers to *Budha*, the Hindu equivalent of Hermes. It could not refer to the historic Buddha, whose death is a known fact, whereas Idrīs is expressly said to have been transported alive to heaven, which corresponds precisely to the biblical Enoch.

11. See *The King of the World*, chap. 3.

among the planetary spheres.[12] It is true that for the Greeks medicine was attributed to Apollo, that is, to the solar principle, and to
his son Asclepius (in Latin, *Aesculapius*); but in the 'Hermetic
books' Asclepius becomes the son of Hermes, and we should also
note that the staff that is his emblem has close symbolic connections
to the caduceus.[13] This example from medicine moreover allows us
to understand how one and the same science can have aspects
related to different orders, thus with equally different correspondences, even if the outward effects obtained are apparently similar,
for there is a purely spiritual or 'theurgic' medicine, and there is also

12. Perhaps it is here that one must see the origin of the error committed by
those who consider the Buddha to be the ninth *avatāra* of Vishnu; in reality this is a
manifestation related to the principle designated as the planetary *Budha*. In this case
the Solar Christ would properly be Glorious Christ, that is, the tenth *avatāra*, who is
to come at the end of the cycle. We will recall as a curiosity that the month of May
takes its name from *Maïa*, Mercury's mother (who is said to be one of the Pleiades)
to whom that month was formerly consecrated in ancient times; now in Christianity it has become the 'month of Mary' by an assimilation, doubtless not merely phonetic, between *Maria* and *Maïa*.

[In his translation of the present chapter included in *The Sword of Gnosis* (Bos-
ton: Arkana, 1986), Martin Lings provides the following expanded version of the
above note, adding that 'it has been somewhat modified by the translator in the light
of conversation that he had with the author many years after the article had been
written':

If Hindu doctrine considers the Buddha as being the ninth *avatāra* of Vishnu,
that is the *Mleccha* (foreign) *avatāra*, this does not necessarily exclude other
divine interventions that have taken place on behalf of 'foreign' (non-Hindu)
peoples during the same period. In particular, Christ might be said to share with
the Buddha the ninth avatāric function, since his first coming was, for the West,
what the advent of the Buddha was for the Far East (and what the Koranic
'descent' was for the 'middle' region). Now, as we have seen in connection with
the Buddha, the ninth *avatāra* is a 'Mercurial' manifestation. It would seem that
the two comings of Christ may be related to his 'Mercurial' and 'Solar' aspects,
the Solar Christ being Christ Glorious, that is, the tenth or *Kalki avatāra*, who is
to come at the end of the cycle, the 'white horse' of this final descent being a solar
symbol par excellence....]

13. Around the staff of Asclepius is coiled a single serpent which represents the
benefic force, for the malefic force must disappear by the very fact that it is a question of the genius of medicine. Let us note too the connection of this same staff of
Asclepius, as an emblem of healing, with the biblical symbol of the 'brazen serpent'
(see on this symbolism our study 'Seth', chap. 22 of *Symbols of Sacred Science*).

Hermetic or 'spagyric' medicine; this is directly related to the question we are presently considering; and perhaps we will explain some day why from the traditional point of view medicine was considered as essentially a sacerdotal science.

On the other hand, there is nearly always a close connection made between Enoch (Idrīs) and Elijah (Dhūl-Kifl), both of whom were taken up to heaven without passing through corporeal death,[14] and Islamic tradition places both in the solar sphere. Similarly, according to the Rosicrucian tradition, *Elias Artista*, who presides over the Hermetic 'Great Work',[15] resides in the 'Solar Citadel', which is the abode of the 'Immortals' (in the sense of the *Chirajīvīs* of Hinduism, that is, beings 'endowed with longevity', whose life lasts throughout the whole cycle),[16] and which represents one of the aspects of the 'Center of the World'. All of this is certainly worthy of reflection, and if one also adds the traditions, which nearly everywhere liken the sun itself symbolically to the fruit of 'the Tree of Life',[17] one will perhaps understand the special relationship which the solar influence has with Hermeticism, insofar as this, like the 'lesser mysteries' of antiquity, has as its essential aim the restoration of the human 'primordial state'. Is this not the 'Solar Citadel' of the Rosicrucians, which is to 'descend from Heaven to earth' at the end of the cycle in the form of the 'Heavenly Jerusalem', realizing the 'squaring of the circle' according to the perfect measure of the 'golden reed'?

14. It is said that they are to appear on earth again at the end of the cycle; they are the two 'witnesses' mentioned in Rev. 11.

15. He incarnates as it were the nature of the 'philosophic fire', and one knows that, according to the Bible narrative, the Prophet Elijah was taken up to heaven on a 'chariot of fire'; this is related to the 'fiery vehicle' (*taijasa* in the Hindu doctrine) which, in the human being, corresponds to the subtle state (see *Man and His Becoming according to the Vedānta*, chap. 14).

16. See *Man and His Becoming according to the Vedānta*, chap. 1. Let us also recall, from the alchemical point of view, the correspondence between the sun and gold, which the Hindu tradition designates as 'mineral light'; the *aurum potabile* of the Hermeticists is moreover the same as the 'draught of immortality', which is also called 'liquor of gold' in Taoism.

17. See *The Symbolism of the Cross*, chap. 9.

3

HERMES' TOMB

WHAT WE HAVE SAID about certain 'pseudo-initiatic' enterprises
makes it easy to understand the reasons why we are very little
inclined to address questions more or less directly touching upon
the ancient Egyptian tradition. On this subject we can even add that
the very fact that present-day Egyptians do not in any way preoccupy themselves with research concerning this vanished civilization
should suffice to show that from the point of view that interests us
there is no effective benefit in doing so. If it were otherwise, it is
quite obvious that they would not have allowed it to be as it were
abandoned to the monopoly of foreigners, who in any case have
never made it anything more than a matter of erudition. The truth
is that between ancient Egypt and present-day Egypt there is no
more than a geographical coincidence without the slightest historical continuity; thus the tradition in question is even more completely foreign in the country where it formerly existed than is
Druidism for the peoples now inhabiting the ancient Celtic coun-
tries; and the fact that many more of its monuments still stand
changes nothing in this respect. We insist on clarifying this point
once and for all in order to cut short all the illusions entertained
only too easily on this subject by those who have never had occasion
to examine things more closely; and at the same time, this statement will destroy yet more completely the claims of 'pseudo-initiates' who, while relying on the evidence of ancient Egypt, would
like to give us to understand that they are connected with something that still subsists in Egypt itself. Moreover, we know that this
is not a purely imaginary supposition, and that some, counting on
general ignorance, in which, unfortunately, they are not altogether
wrong, push their claims to this point.

However, in spite of all this, it so happens that we find ourselves almost obliged to give, insofar as it is possible, some explanations that have lately been asked of us from different quarters as a result of the unbelievable multiplication of certain fantastic stories to which we have been obliged to refer while reviewing the books to which we were alluding just now. Moreover, it must be said that these explanations will not really relate to the Egyptian tradition itself but only to what relates to it in the Arabic tradition. There are at least some rather curious indications that can perhaps contribute in spite of everything to clarifying certain obscure points, although we do not at all intend to exaggerate the importance of the conclusions it is possible to draw from them.

We have pointed out previously that no one really knows what purpose the Great Pyramid served, and we could say the same thing of the pyramids in general. It is true that the most common and widespread opinion is that they were tombs; and doubtless there is nothing impossible in this hypothesis itself. But we also know that because of certain preconceived ideas modern archeologists are resolved to discover tombs everywhere, even where there has never been the slightest trace of them, and this is not without arousing in us some suspicion. In any case, they have yet to find a tomb in the Great Pyramid; but even if one were discovered, the enigma would still not be entirely resolved, for this would obviously not exclude its having other uses at the same time, perhaps even more important ones, just as could other Pyramids that have in fact served as tombs; and it is further possible that, as some have thought, the funerary use of these monuments was a more or less late development, and that this was not their original purpose at the time of their construction. If, however, one objects to this that certain ancient information of a more or less traditional character would seem to confirm that they were really tombs, we will say something which may seem strange at first glance but which is precisely what the considerations to follow will tend to make one admit: are not the tombs in question to be understood in a purely symbolic sense?

Indeed, some say that the Great Pyramid might be the tomb of Idrīs, that is, of the prophet Enoch, while the second Pyramid would be that of another personage who would have been his Master, and of whom we will speak again; but, presented in this way and taken in a literal sense, the thing is manifestly absurd since Enoch did not die but was taken up living to Heaven; how then could he have a tomb? One should not, however, be too hasty to speak here in the Western manner of baseless 'legends', for here is the explanation given: it is not Idrīs' body which was buried in the Pyramid, but his science; by this some understand his books, but what likelihood is there that the books were purely and simply buried, and what interest could this have presented from any point of view?[1] It would assuredly be much more plausible that the contents of these books should have been carved in hieroglyphics on the inside of the monument; but unfortunately for such a supposition there are in fact neither inscriptions nor symbolic figurations of any kind to be found in the Great Pyramid.[2] Therefore there remains only one acceptable hypothesis, which is that Idrīs' science is indeed hidden in the Pyramid, but that it is embedded in its very structure, in its outer and inner arrangement and in its proportions; and everything that may be valid in the 'discoveries' that moderns have made or think they have made on this subject represent in the final analysis only a few minute fragments of this ancient traditional science.

This interpretation agrees quite well moreover with another Arab version of the Pyramids' origin, which attributes their construction to the antediluvian king Surid, who having been warned in a dream of the imminence of the Deluge had the Pyramids built according to the plan of the sages, and ordered the priests to place in them the secrets of their sciences and the precepts of their wisdom. Now we know that Enoch or Idrīs, also antediluvian, is identified with Hermes or Thoth, who represents the source from which the Egyptian priesthood held its knowledge, and so by extension this priesthood

---

1. We hardly need remark that the case of books ritually placed in a true tomb is completely different.

2. On this question we sometimes come across strange and more or less completely fanciful assertions; thus in the *Occult Magazine*, organ of the HB of L, we found an allusion to the 'seventy-eight leaves of the book of Hermes, which lies buried in one of the Pyramids' (Dec. 1885, p87). This is obviously a reference to the Tarot, but this has never been represented as a Book of Hermes, of Thoth, or of Enoch, except in certain very recent conceptions, and it is only as 'Egyptian' as are the Bohemians, to whom this name has also been given. On the 'HB of L', see our book *Theosophy: History of a Pseudo-Religion*. [See also *The Spiritist Fallacy*. ED.]

itself as the continuator of the same function of traditional teaching. It is thus always the same sacred science which in this way too would have been placed in the Pyramids.[3]

On the other hand, this monument destined to assure the preservation of traditional knowledge in anticipation of the cataclysm, recalls yet another well-known story, that of the two columns raised, according to some, precisely by Enoch, and according to others by Seth, on which the essentials of all the sciences was inscribed; and the mention made here of Seth leads us back to the personage for whom the second Pyramid is reputed to have been the tomb. Indeed, if this was the Master of Idrīs, he could not have been any other than Shīth, that is, Seth, son of Adam. It is true that some ancient Arab authors call him by the apparently strange names of *Aghatīmūn* and *Adhīmūn*, but these are visibly only deformations of the Greek *Agathodaemon*, which, relating back to the symbolism of the serpent envisaged under its benefic aspect, applies perfectly to Seth, as we have explained elsewhere.[4] The particular connection thus established between Seth and Enoch is all the more remarkable in that both are also connected with certain traditions concerning a return to the Terrestrial Paradise, that is, to the 'primordial state', and consequently with a 'polar' symbolism that is not unconnected with the orientation of the Pyramids. But this is another question, and we will only note in passing that this fact, which implies clearly enough a reference to 'spiritual centers', would tend to confirm the hypothesis that makes of the Pyramids a place of initiation, which, moreover, would have been the normal way to keep 'alive' the knowledge enclosed in it, at least as long as this initiation subsisted.

---

3. Still another version, no longer Arab but Coptic, attributes the origin of the Pyramids to Shedīd and Sheddād, the sons of Ad. We really do not know what conclusions could be drawn from this, and it does not seem that there is reason to attach any great importance to it, for besides the fact that it is a question of 'giants' here, we do not see what symbolic intention it could conceal.

4. See our study 'Seth', chap. 22 of *Symbols of Sacred Science*. The *Agathodaemon* of the Greeks is often identified with Kneph, also represented by the serpent in connection with the 'World Egg', which always refers to the same symbolism. As for the *Kakodaemon*, the malefic aspect of the serpent, it is evidently identical to the Set-Typhon of the Egyptians.

Let us add that it is said that Idrīs or Enoch wrote many inspired books after Adam himself and Seth had already written others;[5] these books were the prototypes of the sacred books of the Egyptians, and the more recent *Hermetic Books* represent only as it were a 'readaptation' of them, as is also the case with the various *Books of Enoch* that have come down to us under this name. On the other hand, the books of Adam, Seth, and Enoch naturally have expressed different aspects of traditional knowledge, each implying a particular relationship with one or another of the sacred sciences, as is always the case for the teaching transmitted by the different Prophets. It might be interesting in these conditions to ask with regard to Enoch and Seth whether there ought not to be something corresponding to these differences in the structure of the two Pyramids we spoke of, and whether perhaps the third Pyramid would not likewise have some connection with Adam, for although we have not found any explicit allusion to this anywhere, it would after all be quite logical to suppose that it ought to complete the ternary of the great antediluvian Prophets.[6] Of course, we do not at all think that these questions are resolvable at present; besides, all modern 'seekers' have, so to speak, been 'hypnotized' almost exclusively by the Great Pyramid, although it is really not so much larger than the other two that the difference is striking. And when, in order to justify the exceptional importance they attribute to it, they maintain that it is the only one which was oriented exactly, perhaps they are making the error of not considering that certain variations in orientation might well be due not simply to some negligence on the part of the builders, but reflect precisely something connected to different traditional 'epochs'. But how could one expect modern Westerners to be guided in their researches by even the least accurate and appropriate ideas on things of this sort?[7]

5. The numbers of these books varies and in many cases may be only symbolic, but this point has only a rather secondary importance.

6. It goes without saying that this does not mean that the construction of the Pyramids must be literally attributed to them, but only that it may have constituted a 'fixation' of the traditional sciences respectively linked to them.

7. The idea that the Great Pyramid differs essentially from the other two seems very recent. It is said that the Caliph Al-Mamūn, wishing to ascertain what the Pyramids contained, decided to have one opened; this happened to be the Great Pyramid, but he does not seem to have thought it was at all special in character.

Another observation which also has its importance is that the very name Hermes is far from being unknown to the Arab tradition;[8] should we see only a 'coincidence' in the similarity that it presents with the word *Haram* (*Ahrām* in the plural), an Arab designation for the Pyramid, from which it differs only by the addition of a final letter that is not a part of its root? Hermes is called *Al-muthalleh bil-hikam*, literally 'triple by wisdom',[9] which is equivalent to the Greek epithet *Trismegistus*, although it is more explicit, for the 'greatness' which this last expresses is at root really only the result of the wisdom that is the proper attribute of Hermes.[10] Moreover, this 'triplicity' has still another meaning, for it is sometimes found elaborated in the form of three distinct Hermes: the first, called 'Hermes of Hermes' (*Hermes Al-Harāmesah*) and considered antediluvian, is properly identified with Idrīs; the two others, who would be postdiluvian, are the 'Babylonian Hermes' (*Al-Bābelī*) and the 'Egyptian Hermes' (*Al-Misrī*). This seems to indicate quite clearly that the Chaldean and Egyptian traditions were derived directly from one and the same principal source, which, given its acknowledged antediluvian character, can hardly have been other than the Atlantean tradition.[11]

Whatever one may think of all these considerations, which are certainly as far from the views of Egyptologists as they are from

8. In addition to the correct form *Hermes*, we also find in certain authors the form *Armis*, which is obviously a distortion of it.

9. *Hikam* is the plural of *hikmah*, but both the singular and the plural forms are used in the sense of 'wisdom'.

10. It is curious to note that the word *muthalleth* also designates the triangle, for one could, without forcing things too much, find in it a link with the triangular form of the Pyramid's faces, which must also have been determined 'by the wisdom' of those who designed them, and this without taking into account that the triangle is also linked to the symbolism of the 'Pole'; and from this last point of view it is quite evident that the Pyramid itself is in fact only one image of the 'sacred Mountain'.

11. It is easy to understand that all this is already rather remote from the primordial tradition, and there would in any case be very little point in specially designating the latter as the common source of two particular traditions, since it is necessarily the source of all traditional forms without exception. One could however conclude from the order of enumeration of the three Hermes that, insofar as it seems to have some chronological significance, the Chaldean tradition had a certain anteriority with respect to the Egyptian tradition.

those of the modern investigators of the 'secret of the Pyramid', it is permissible to say that this truly represents 'Hermes' tomb', for the mysteries of his wisdom and his science have been concealed in it in such a way that it is certainly very difficult to find them.[12]

12. While on this subject, we will point out yet another modern fantasy. We have noted that some attribute a considerable importance to the fact that the Great Pyramid was never finished; indeed the top is missing, but all we can say for certain here is that the most ancient authors whose testimony we have, and who are still relatively recent, always saw it truncated as it is today. To claim from this that the missing summit corresponds to the 'corner stone' spoken of in the Bible and in the Gospel is really going too far, all the more because according to much more authentically traditional information, the stone in question would not be a 'pyramidion' but rather a 'keystone', and if it was 'rejected by the builders', it is because these, being initiated only into *Square Masonry*, were ignorant of the secrets of *Arch Masonry*. Another curious thing is that the seal of the United States portrays a truncated pyramid above which is a radiating triangle which, while being separate and even isolated by the circle of clouds surrounding it, seems to replace the summit; but there are also in this seal, which certain 'pseudo-initiatic' organizations seek to profit from, other details that are, to say the least, bizarre. Thus, the thirteen courses of the pyramid are said to correspond to the thirteen tribes of Israel (counting the two half-tribes of the sons of Joseph separately), and this is perhaps not altogether unrelated to the real origins of certain contemporary ramblings about the Great Pyramid, which tend to make of it, for rather obscure reasons, a sort of Judeo-Christian monument.

REVIEWS

Enel: *Les Origines de la Genèse et l'enseignement des Temples de l'ancienne Egypte.* vol. 1, 1re et 2e parties. (Cairo: Institut français d'Archéologie orientale, 1935). It is assuredly very difficult, and perhaps even wholly impossible today, to know what the ancient Egyptian tradition, extinct for so many centuries, really was. Thus, the various interpretations and reconstructions attempted by Egyptologists are largely hypothetical and, moreover, often contradict each other. The present work is distinguished from the usual Egyptological works by a laudable concern for doctrinal comprehension which is generally absent from them, and also by the great importance it rightly gives to symbolism, which the 'official' scholars for their part tend to deny or to ignore purely and simply; but is this to say that the views expressed here are less hypothetical than the others? We rather doubt this, especially seeing that they are inspired by a sort of prejudice toward finding a constant parallelism between the Egyptian and Hebraic traditions, for although the basis is essentially the same everywhere, nothing proves that the two forms in question have truly been so close to one another, and the direct filiation which the author seems to imagine between them and which the title itself probably means to suggest, is more than contestable. From this result more or less forced assimilations; it must be asked, for example, whether it is really certain that the Egyptian doctrine considered universal manifestation under the aspect of 'creation', which seems so peculiar to the Hebraic tradition and to those that are linked to it. The testimony of the ancients, who ought to have known better than we what they believed, does not support it in any way; and on this point our suspicion increases further when we note that the same principle is sometimes called 'Creator' and sometimes simply 'Demiurge'; one must at least choose between these two obviously incompatible roles... On the other hand, the linguistic considerations put forward doubtless call for many reservations as well, for the language in which the Egyptian tradition expresses itself is no better known than is that tradition itself; and we should add that some interpretations are clearly too much influenced by occultist ideas. But despite everything, this is not to say that there is not in this volume, whose first part is devoted to the Universe and the second to Man, a fairly great number of remarks worthy of interest, of which some could even be confirmed by comparison with the Eastern traditions, which unfortunately the author seems to ignore almost completely, much better than by biblical references. Naturally, we cannot enter into details here; to give one example, we will only point out, in this order of ideas, what is said concerning the constellation of the Thigh, a designation of the 'Great Bear', and the expression 'Master of the Thigh', which applies to the Pole. There would be some curious connections to point out here. Finally, let us note the opinion of the author on the Great Pyramid, which he sees as both a 'Solar Temple' and a monument to 'immortalize the knowledge of the laws of the Universe.' This supposition is at least as plausible as many others that have been put forward on the subject; but as for saying that 'the hidden symbolism of the Hebrew and Christian Scriptures relates directly to facts which took place during the construction of the Great Pyramid,' this is an assertion which seems to us to lack plausibility in every respect!

ENEL: *A Message from the Sphinx* (London: Rider & Co., 1936). The reservations we expressed last year in connection with another work of the same author as to the purely hypothetical character of all attempts at the reconstitution and interpretation of the ancient Egyptian tradition apply equally to this one, where we find once again in the first part, treated more briefly, some of the same ideas. The book opens with a study of hieroglyphic writing based on perfectly sound principles, which are moreover quite generally known, concerning the plurality of meanings of this writing. But when these are to be applied in detail, how can we really be certain not to mix in a greater or lesser measure of fantasy? Let us also note that the term 'ideographic' does not apply, as is claimed, to the simple representation of sensible objects, and that when it is a question of writing it is in short synonymous with 'symbolic'; and there are many other improprieties of language which are no less regrettable. For example, it is quite certain that the Egyptian doctrine must have been at root 'monotheistic', for all traditional doctrines without exception are so in the sense that they cannot but affirm principial unity. But if the word 'monotheism' thus has an acceptable meaning, even outside of specifically religious forms, has one the right to call 'pantheism' what everyone else is accustomed to call 'polytheism'? Another more serious error concerns magic, which the author clearly confuses in many cases with theurgy (a confusion which amounts in the final analysis to that between the psychic and the spiritual), for he sees it wherever the 'power of the word' is involved, which leads him to believe that it must have had a major role at the very beginning, whereas on the contrary its predominance, as we have often explained, could only have been in Egypt, as elsewhere, a more or less late degeneration also. Let us note before going further a rather unfortunate concession made to modern 'evolutionist' theories: if the men of those ancient times possessed the crude or rudimentary mentality ascribed to them, where could they ever have recruited those 'initiates' in whom, at the same time, one observes precisely the opposite? One must necessarily choose between anti-traditional 'evolutionism' and the acceptance of traditional facts, and any compromise can only lead to insoluble contradictions.

The second part of the book is devoted to the Hebrew Kabbalah, which might be surprising if we were not already familiar with the ideas of the author on this subject. For him the Hebrew tradition is directly descended from the Egyptian tradition; they are like 'two consecutive links of the same chain.' We have already said what we think about this, but we will clarify the point further: the author is certainly right when he says that the Egyptian tradition was derived from Atlantis (which, we can say more clearly than he does, was not therefore itself the seat of the primordial tradition), but it was not the only one. And the same thing seems true particularly of the Chaldean tradition; the Arab teaching on the 'three Hermes', of which we spoke elsewhere, shows this descent quite clearly. But, if the principal source is thus the same, the difference of these forms was probably determined by the meeting with other currents, one coming from the South in the case of Egypt, and the other from the North in that of Chaldea. Now the Hebrew tradition is essentially 'Abrahamic', hence of Chaldean origin; the 'readaptation' effected by Moses was no doubt able, because of circumstances of place, to make accessory use of Egyptian elements, especially as regards certain more or less secondary traditional sciences; but it could never have had the effect of causing this tradition to depart from its own lineage so as to transfer it into another lineage foreign to the people for whom it was expressly destined and in whose language it had to be formulated. Besides, as soon as one recognizes the common origin and foundation of all traditional doctrines, the observation of certain similarities does not in any way imply a direct filiation; this is the case for example with links like those the author wishes to establish between the *Sephiroth* and the Egyptian 'Ennead', assuming that they are justified; and strictly speaking, even if the resemblances seem to be based on points too particular to go back as far as the primordial tradition, the kinship of the Egyptian and Chaldean traditions would in any case amply suffice to explain it. As for claiming that primitive Hebraic writing was derived from hieroglyphs, this is an entirely gratuitous hypothesis, since no one in fact knows exactly what this writing was; all the indications that one can find concerning them tend rather to make one think the contrary; moreover, it is not at all clear how the association of numbers with letters, which is essential for Hebrew, could really have been borrowed from the hieroglyphic system. What is more, the close similarities between Hebrew and Arabic, to which not the least allusion is made here, clearly runs counter to this hypothesis, for it would be very difficult to seriously maintain that the Arab tradition also had to come from Egypt!

We will pass rapidly over the third part, where we first find views on art which, if they do in spite of everything contain some truth, nonetheless still start from an affirmation that is questionable at the very least; it is not possible to say, at least without more clarification, that 'there is only one art', for it is obvious that the underlying unity, namely ideas expressed symbolically, in no way excludes the multiplicity of forms. In the chapters that follow the author gives a survey, not of authentic traditional sciences as one might wish, but of more or less distorted fragments that have survived until our time, especially under the 'divinatory' aspect; the influence of 'occultist' conceptions appear here in a particularly regrettable way. Let us state once again that it is wholly inaccurate to say that certain sciences taught in the temples of antiquity were purely and simply equivalent to modern 'academic' sciences; in reality, even where there is an apparent similarity of object, the point of view was still totally different, and there is always a veritable abyss between the traditional sciences and the profane sciences. Finally, we cannot refrain from pointing out some errors of detail that are truly astonishing; thus the well known image of the 'churning of the sea' is said to be that of a 'god, Samudra Mutu' [*sic*]! But this is perhaps still more excusable than the errors about things which should be more familiar to the author than the Hindu tradition, particularly the Hebrew language. We will not speak of mere errors of transcription, although this is terribly careless; but how can one continually call *Ain Bekar* that which is really *Aiq Bekar* (a cryptographic system that is as well-known in Arabic as in Hebrew, where one can find the prototype of the Masonic alphabets), confuse the final form of *kaph* with that of *nun* with regard to their numerical value, and even mention a 'final *samek*', which has never existed and which is nothing but a *mem*? How can one insist that the translators of Genesis have rendered *tehōm* by 'waters', in a place where the word in the Hebrew text is *maim* and not *thehōm*, or that *Ain Soph* literally means the 'Ancient of Years' when the strictly literal translation of this name is 'without limit'? *Yetsirah* is 'Formation' and not 'Creation' (which is *Beriah*); *Zohar* does not mean 'celestial Chariot' (an obvious confusion with the *Merkabah*) but 'Splendor'; and the author seems to be wholly ignorant of what the *Talmud* is, since he thinks it is formed from the *Notarikon*, the *Temourah*, and the *Gematria*, which however are not 'books', as he says, but kabbalistic methods of interpretation! We shall stop here, but it will be agreed that such errors hardly encourage one to blindly accept the author's assertions on less easily verifiable points and to grant an unreserved confidence to his Egyptological theories...

XAVIER GUICHARD: *Eleusis Alésia: Enquête sur les origenes de la civilisation européene* (Abbeville: F. Paillart, 1936). Whatever one may think of the views expressed in this work, it is nonetheless fitting to pay tribute to the work it represents, and to the patience and perseverance shown by the author, who for more than twenty years dedicated to this research all the spare time left him by his professional duties. He has studied all the places, not only in France but in all of Europe, with a name that seems to be derived, sometimes under rather altered forms, from *Alesia*. He has found a considerable number of these, and has noticed that all share certain common topographical particularities: they 'occupy sites surrounded by more or less important water courses which isolate them almost into islands', and 'all possess a mineral spring.' From a 'prehistoric' or at the very least 'proto-historic' epoch, these 'alesian sites' were chosen, because of their privileged locations, as 'meeting-places' (this is the original meaning of their name) and soon became centers of habitation, which would seem to be confirmed by the numerous traces generally found there. In short, all of this is perfectly plausible, and only shows that in those regions what is called 'civilization' goes back very much further than is ordinarily supposed, and that since that time there has not been any real interruption. But we do have reservations about the assimilation of certain names; even that of *Alesia* with *Eleusis* is not as obvious as the author seems to believe, and in general it is regrettable that certain of his speculations bear witness to insufficient or unsure linguistic knowledge on many points; but even leaving the more doubtful cases aside, there still remain enough, especially in Western Europe, to justify what we have just said. Moreover, it goes without saying that the existence of this ancient 'civilization' does not in any way surprise us, whatever its origin and characteristics may have been—questions to which we shall return later.

But there is still something else which seems even more extraordinary: the author has noted that the 'alesian sites' were regularly laid out according to lines radiating from a center and running from one end of Europe to the other; he has found twenty four such lines, which he calls 'alesian itineraries', and which all converge on Mount Poupet near Alaise, at the Doubs.[13] Besides this system of geodesic lines there is even a second system formed by a 'meridian', an 'equinoctial', and two 'solstitials', whose center is in another point of the same 'alesia', marked by a place with the name of Myon. And there is even a series of 'alesian sites' (some of which coincide with the preceding ones) marking out lines that correspond exactly to the different degrees of longitude and latitude. All this forms a rather complex ensemble, and unfortunately it cannot be said that everything seems to be absolutely rigorous. Thus the twenty-four lines of the first system do not all form equal angles; moreover, one needs only a very slight error of direction in the starting-point in order to have a considerable deviation at a certain distance, something that leaves a rather larger degree of 'approximation'; there are also isolated 'alesian sites' outside of these lines, hence exceptions or anomalies... On the other hand, it is hard to see what the special importance of the central 'alesia' can have been; it is possible that it really did have one at some distant period, but it is rather astonishing that no trace of it has survived apart from a few 'legends' which are in no way exceptional, and which are also associated with many other places. In any case, this is

13. A river in eastern France. ED.

an unresolved question that in the present state of things is perhaps even insoluble. Be that as it may, there is another more serious objection which the author has not considered and which is as follows: on the one hand, as we saw earlier, the 'alesian sites' are defined by certain conditions that relate to the natural configuration of the terrain; on the other hand, they are situated on lines which were traced artificially by the men of a certain age: how can these two things of a wholly different order be reconciled? The 'alesian sites' thus have as it were two distinct definitions, and it is hard to see how they can be reconciled; at the very least this calls for an explanation, and as long as one is looking it must be recognized that all of this has a certain air of improbability. It would be different if one were to say that most of the places showing 'alesian' characteristics were naturally distributed according to certain determinate patterns; this might be strange, but not impossible, for it is possible that the world is really much more 'geometric' than is thought; and in this case, people would only have had to recognize the existence of these lines and to transform them into roads linking their different 'alesian' establishments; if the lines in question are not a simple 'cartographic' illusion, we hardly see how they can be accounted for otherwise.

We have just spoken of roads, and it is really this which implies the existence on the 'alesian itineraries' of certain 'distance markers' consisting of places most of which bear names like Calais, Versailles, Myon, and Millières. The distances of these places from the center are exact multiples of a unit of measure to which the author gives the conventional name 'alesian stadium'; and what is particularly remarkable is that this unit, which would have been the prototype of the Greek stadium, the Roman mile, and the Gallic league, is equal to the sixth part of a degree, which implies that the men who determined its length knew with precision the true dimensions of the terrestrial sphere. On this subject, the author points to facts indicating that the knowledge possessed by the geographers of 'classical' antiquity such as Strabo and Ptolemy, far from being the result of their own discoveries, represented the remnants of a much more ancient or even 'prehistoric' science, of which the greater part had by then been lost. What is astonishing is that in spite of such acknowledgments, he accepts the 'evolutionist' theories on which 'prehistory' such as is taught 'officially' is built. Whether he truly accepts them or simply does not dare risk contradicting them, there is something in his attitude which is not entirely logical and which greatly weakens his thesis. In fact, this aspect of the question can only be clarified by the idea of traditional sciences, and this appears nowhere in this study; there is not the least suspicion that there even existed a science whose origin was other than 'empirical' and which was not formed 'progressively' by a long series of observations by means of which man is supposed to have emerged little by little from a so-called 'primitive' ignorance, which is here simply carried back a little further into the past than is common.

Of course the same lack of any traditional information also affects the way the origin of the 'alesian civilization' is envisaged; the truth is that at the beginning, and even much later, all things had a ritual and 'sacred' character; thus there is no need to ask whether 'religious' influences (an inappropriate word in any case) affected this or that particular point, a question which comes from an all too modern point of view and sometimes even has the effect of completely revers-ing certain relationships. Thus, even if it is conceded that the designa-tion 'Champs-Elysées' is related to the 'alesian' names (which seems rather hypothetical), one cannot conclude that the abode of the dead was conceived after the model of the inhabited areas near which the bodies were buried, but on the contrary, that these places themselves were chosen or arranged in conformity with the ritual exigencies gov-erned by that idea, which at that time certainly counted for much more than simple 'utilitarian' preoccupations, even if these latter really existed as such at a time when human life was entirely regulated by traditional knowledge. On the other hand, it is possible that the 'elysian myths' were connected with 'chthonian' cults (and what we have explained about the symbolism of the cave would even explain in certain cases their relationship with the initiatic 'mysteries'), but again it would have been appropriate to explain more fully the meaning attributed to this assertion. In any case, the 'Mother-Goddess' was undoubtedly something quite different than 'Nature', unless by this are understood *Natura naturans*, which is no longer a 'naturalist' con-ception at all. We must add that a predominance given to the 'Mother-Goddess' does not seem to go back beyond the beginning of the *Kali-Yuga*, of which it is quite a clear characteristic; and this perhaps allows one to 'date' the 'alesian civilization' more exactly, that is, to determine the cyclic period to which it must be connected. Here there is assur-edly something earlier than 'history' in the ordinary sense of the word, but nonetheless already very far removed from the true origins.

Finally, the author seems bent on establishing that 'European civilization' had its origin in Europe itself, apart from any foreign influences, especially Eastern ones; but this is not really how the question should be put. We know that the primordial origin of tradition, and accordingly of all 'civilization', was in fact hyperborean, and neither Eastern nor Western; but at the age in question, it is evident that one can envisage a secondary current that more directly gave birth to this 'alesian civilization', and in fact various indications make us think especially here of the Atlantean current during the period when it was spreading from West to East after the disappearance of Atlantis itself. Of course this is only a suggestion, but it is one that at least is able to include in the framework of traditional data all that can justifiably be based on the results of those investigations. In any case, there is no doubt that a question such as that of the 'alesian sites' can only be treated completely and accurately from the point of view of 'sacred geography'; but it must be said that among the ancient traditional sciences, the reconstruction of this science would today raise altogether insurmountable difficulties; and in the presence of certain enigmas encountered in this domain, one may wonder whether, even during periods where no notable cataclysm occurred, the 'countenance' of the terrestrial world has not sometimes changed in a very strange way.

NÖEL DE LA HOUSSAYE: *Les Bronzes italiotes archaiques et leur symbolique.* (Paris: Éditions du Trident, 1938). This study begins with a consideration of the origins of coinage in the Mediterranean basin, a rather obscure subject for which, as for so many other things, it does not seem possible to go back beyond the sixth century BC. In any case, the author understands well enough that 'for the ancients coinage was a sacred thing', contrary to the wholly profane conception that the moderns have of it—and that this explains the character of the symbols which it bore; one could go even further, we think, and see these symbols as the mark of control exercised by a spiritual authority. What follows more particularly concerns Rome and Italy, and is much more hypothetical: relating the name of Aeneas to the Latin name for bronze [*aeneus*], that even if not impossible, seems rather questionable; and it is perhaps a rather restricted interpretation of the legend of Aeneas to see in the different stages of his journeys nothing more than the spread of bronze coinage. Whatever importance this may have had, however, it can only be a secondary fact, doubtless linked to an entire tradition. Be that as it may, what seems to us most improbable is the idea that the Aeneas legend can have any connection with Atlantis. To begin with, Aeneas's journeys from Asia Minor to Italy obviously do not have their starting-point in the West; next, they refer to a time which, even if it cannot be precisely determined, is in any event several thousand years after the disappearance of Atlantis. But this over-imaginative theory, as well as some linguistic fantasies on which we shall not dwell, must probably be attributed to the fact that the study in question first appeared in part in the journal *Atlantis*...

The enumeration of the symbols figuring on the coins seems to be as complete as possible, and synoptic tables have been added at the end of the work that allow one to see their distribution on the circumference of the Mediterranean basin; but there could have been much more to say on the meaning of these symbols, and in this respect there are indeed some quite astonishing gaps. Thus, we do not understand how one can say that the prow of a ship associated with the figure of Janus on the Roman *as*,[14] 'concerns Saturn, and him alone,' when it is quite well known that the ship or the barque was one of the attributes of Janus himself; and it is curious too that with regard to Saturn, what is called the 'pastoral era' is really the 'agricultural era', that is to say exactly the opposite, since the shepherds are essentially nomadic peoples while the farmers are sedentary. How then could the 'pastoral era' really coincide with the 'formation of towns'? What is said of the Dioscuri[15] scarcely clarifies the meaning, and the same goes for the Kabiri.[16] But above all, how is it that the author does not seem to have observed that the symbolism of the latter is closely related to metallurgy, and even more particularly to copper, something which would have had a direct bearing on his subject?

NÖEL DE LA HOUSSAYE: *Le Phoenix, poème symbolique.* (Paris: Éditions du Trident, n.d.). We are not qualified to appraise a poem as such, but, from the symbolic point of view this poem seems to us less

---

14. A unit of money. ED.

15. The twins Castor and Pollux. ED.

16. A group of deities whose primary worship was in Samothrace, associated especially with Hephaestus as being master metal workers. ED.

clear than might be hoped, and even the essentially 'cyclic' and 'solar' character of the myth of the phoenix does not emerge very clearly; as for the symbol of the egg, we confess that we have not managed to grasp how it is envisaged here. In spite of its title, the inspiration of the whole gives the impression of being more 'philosophical' than symbolic; on the other hand, the author appears to seriously believe in the existence of an organization called the 'Brothers of Heliopolis' and in its links with an Egyptian tradition. Europeans do have rather curious ideas about Egypt... Moreover, is he quite sure that it is the Heliopolis in Egypt with which the phoenix was originally associated? There was also a Heliopolis in Syria, and if one recalls that the region of Syria did not always coincide exactly with the country that bears this name today, this can bring us nearer to its origins. The truth, in fact, is that these various relatively recent 'Cities of the Sun' were only secondary images of the hyperborean 'solar earth', and thus, beyond all the derivative forms that are 'historically' known, the symbolism of the phoenix is directly linked to the primordial tradition itself.

Lettres d'Humanité (Paris: Societé d'éditions 'Le Belles Lettres', ser. 1942–45). *Lettres d'Humanité*, a publication of L'Association Guillaume Budé, contains in its third volume (1944) a curious essay by Paul Maury entitled *Le Secret de Virgile et l'architecture des Bucoliques*. The author in fact has discovered there a veritable 'architecture', almost as astonishing as that of the *Divine Comedy*. It would be difficult to summarize all this, but we shall try to point out at least its principal features. Firstly he has noticed a symmetry between eclogues I and IX (the ordeals of the Earth), II and VIII (the ordeals of Love), III and VII (the liberating Music), and IV and VI (the supernatural Revelations); these eight eclogues form a double progression, ascending for the first four and descending for the last four, that is to say a sort of double ladder whose summit is occupied by eclogue V (Daphnis), which he calls 'the Bucolic major'. There remains eclogue X (Gallus), which is opposed to eclogue V 'as profane love is opposed to sacred love, as is the imperfectly initiated man of flesh to the ideal of man reformed'; these are 'the two limits between which the souls circulate, between the terraqueous globe and Olympus.' The whole thus forms the plan of a kind of 'chapel', or rather of a 'Pythagorean basilica', of which eclogue V constitutes the apse while eclogue X is at the opposite extremity; between the two the other eclogues are ranged laterally on one side and the other, those which are in symmetry naturally facing each other. But this is not all, and the remarks which follow are even more extraordinary. These refer to the number of the verses of the different eclogues, in which are found other multiple symmetries which certainly can only be intentional. At first glance, it is true, a few of these numerical symmetries appear to be only approximate; but the slight differences thus noted have led the author to work out and 'localize' certain alterations of the text (verses omitted or added), but these are very few in any event and coincide precisely with those which had already been suspected for purely philological reasons. That done, the symmetries all become exact; unfortunately, it is not possible for us to reproduce here the various tables in which these symmetries are presented and without which they can hardly be comprehensible. We will only say, therefore, that the principal numbers evident here and which are repeated with an emphasis that is significant, are 183 (a number by which, according to a passage from Plutarch, 'the Pythagoreans represented the harmony of the great Cosmos itself'), 333, and 666; the last is also 'a Pythagorean number, a triangular number of 36, itself a triangle of 8, the double Ogdoad of the Tetrad'; we shall add that this is essentially a 'solar' number, and point out that the meaning attributed to it in the Apocalypse does not constitute a 'reversal of values' as the author says, but really represents an application of the opposite aspect of that number, which possesses itself, as do so many other symbols, both a 'benefic' and a 'malefic' meaning. It was obviously the first of these two meanings that Virgil had in view; now is it correct to say that he wished particularly to make the number 666 'the cipher of Caesar', which would appear to be confirmed by the fact that, according to the commentator Servius, the Daphnis of the central eclogue v would be none other than Caesar himself? There is certainly nothing implausible in this, and other rather remarkable parallels are invoked in support of this interpretation. Let us add that this cannot be seen as a mere 'political' application in the ordinary sense of the word, if one thinks of the not even exclusively 'religious' side of Caesar (which the author recognizes) but of his truly 'esoteric' role. We cannot pursue this question any further, but we think we have said enough to show the value of this work, and we particularly recommend it to those interested in the symbolism of numbers.

In the same publication, other articles devoted to Hippocrates call for a few remarks. Much is presently being said in medical circles of a 'return to Hippocrates', but strangely enough this seems to be viewed in two different and even contrary ways, for while some understand it, and rightly so, in the sense of a restoration of traditional ideas, others, as is the case here, would like to turn it altogether into its opposite. The latter would attribute to Hippocratic medicine a 'philosophical' character, that is, according to the meaning they give to the word 'rationalist', even a 'secular' character (do they forget then that Hippocrates himself came from a priestly family, failing which he could not have been a physician?), and with this as justification oppose it to the ancient sacerdotal medicine, in which they naturally see, in conformity with the customary modern prejudice, only 'empiricism' and 'superstition'! We do not believe it pointless to draw this to the attention of the partisans of traditional Hippocratism and to urge them, when the occasion arises, to set things right and to react against this unfortunate interpretation. It would be truly regrettable to allow a movement which, even if as yet it indicates no more than a tendency, is certainly not lacking in interest from more than one point of view, to be diverted from its normal and legitimate aim.

Lettres d'Humanité, volume four (1945) contains a long study of Pierre Grimal's *Le Dieu Janus et les origines de Rome*, where there are found many interesting and little known historical facts, although unfortunately no really important conclusions can be drawn from them. The author is certainly right in criticizing the 'historians of religions' who wish to reduce everything to 'ideas' as 'simple and crude' as those of 'forces of nature' or 'social functions'; but are his own explanations, even if more subtle, really any more satisfactory? Whatever one might think of the more or less hypothetical existence of an ancient word *ianus*, meaning the 'action of going' and consequently having the meaning of 'passage', we do not see how this allows one to maintain that there was originally no relationship between this word and the name of the god Janus, for a simple difference of declension most certainly does not prevent their sharing a common root; in truth, these are nothing but philological subtleties with no serious import. Even if one admits that the name of Janus was initially not Latin (because, for Grimal, Janus would have been first and foremost a 'foreign god'), why would the root *i*, 'to go', which is common to Latin and Sanskrit, not be found in other languages? Another rather plausible hypothesis could still be put forward: why could not the Romans, when they adopted this god, have translated his name, whatever it may have been, by an equivalent in their own language, just as they later changed the names of the Greek gods in order to assimilate them to their own? In sum, Grimal's thesis is that the ancient Janus could never have been a 'door god', and that this attribute would have been attached to him only 'belatedly', as a result of a confusion between two words which were quite different although quite similar in form. But all this does not seem at all convincing to us, for the assumption of a so-called 'fortuitous' coincidence never explains anything. Moreover, it is obvious that the deeper significance of the symbolism of the 'door god' escapes him; has he even noticed its close connection with the role of Janus in the annual cycle, which nevertheless brings him back quite directly to the fact that this same Janus was, as he says, a 'god of Heaven' as well as a god of initiation? This last point, moreover, is passed over entirely in silence; it is well said, however, that 'Janus was an initiator, the very god of initiators,' but this term is taken there only in an indirect and wholly profane sense which in reality has absolutely nothing to do with initiation... Some rather curious remarks are made on a god *Bifrons* existing elsewhere than in Rome, especially in the eastern basin of the Mediterranean, but it is very much out of proportion to wish to conclude from this that 'in Rome Janus is only the incarnation of a Syrian Uranus,' since, as we have often said, similarities between different traditions are very far from necessarily implying 'borrowings' from the one to the other. But can one ever make this understood to those who believe that the 'historical method' is applicable to everything?

In the same volume there is an article entitled 'Béatrice dans la vie et l'oeuvre de Dante' which does not present any interest from our point of view, but which does call for a remark: how is it possible, after the appearance of so many works on the *Fedeli d'Amore* written by Luigi Valli and many others, that one can be ignorant when dealing with Dante (or at least affect such ignorance) of the existence of an esoteric and initiatic significance? The only allusion here is to the theological interpretation by R.P. Mandonnet, which is certainly quite insufficient but which, although wholly exoteric, at least acknowledges a meaning higher than the crude 'literalism' which only sees in

Beatrice 'a woman of flesh and blood'. Nevertheless, this 'literalism' is still upheld as lending itself to 'a more psychological and more human explanation,' that is to say, in short, one more to the taste of the moderns and more in conformity with 'esthetic' and 'literary' prejudices which were quite foreign to Dante and his contemporaries!

GEORGES DUMÉZIL: *L'Héritage indo-européen à Rome* (Paris: Gallimard, 1949). Dumézil set out from an altogether secular point of view, but in the course of his researches he came across certain traditional data from which he drew conclusions which are not without interest but which are not always entirely justified and should not be accepted without reservations, all the more so as he almost always tries to support them with linguistic considerations of which the least that can be said is that they are very hypothetical. Furthermore, as the data is necessarily very fragmentary, he has 'fastened' exclusively and as it were systematically on certain things such as the 'tripartite' division, which he insists on finding everywhere, and which in fact does exist in many cases, but which is not the only one to be taken into account here, even if we confine ourselves to his specialized domain. In this volume he has undertaken to sum up the present state of his labors, for it must be recognized that he at least does not claim to have succeeded in reaching any final results, and moreover his continuing discoveries have already led him to modify his conclusions on several occasions. What is essentially involved here is the sifting out of those elements in the Roman tradition which appear to go back directly to the epoch when the peoples called by common consent 'Indo-European' had not yet split into distinct branches which thereafter existed independently of the others. The basis of his theory is the ternary of divinities consisting of Jupiter, Mars, and Quirinus,[17] which he regards as corresponding to three social functions; moreover, he seems to try rather too hard to reduce everything to the social point of view, which easily risks leading to a reversal of the real relationships between principles and their applications. With him there is even a certain rather 'juridical' turn of mind which obviously limits his horizon; we do not know whether he acquired this because he devoted himself primarily to the

---

17. A Roman god of war similar to Mars, but later identified with the deified Romulus. ED.

study of the Roman civilization, or on the contrary because, already having this tendency, Roman civilization particularly attracted him, but in any case the two do not seem entirely unconnected. We cannot enter here into the details of the questions treated in this book, but we must at the very least point out a truly curious remark, all the more so because upon it a great part of these considerations rest. This is that many accounts of events presented elsewhere as 'myths' are found again, with all their principal features, in what is given as the history of the first days of Rome, whence it should be concluded that the Romans transformed into 'ancient history' what was really originally their 'mythology'. To judge from the examples Dumézil gives it does appear that there is some truth in this, although one should perhaps not misuse this interpretation by generalizing it beyond measure. It is true that one could also ask whether history, especially 'sacred history', may not in certain cases indeed reproduce the myth and offer a 'humanized' image of it; but it goes without saying that such a question, which in short is none other than that of the symbolic value of historical facts, cannot even occur to the modernist spirit.

LIST OF ORIGINAL SOURCES

V. I. = Le Voile d'Isis, E. T. = Études Traditionnelles

PT. I, 1.	*E. T.* Oct. 1938
REVIEWS	M. Eliade, *E. T.* Dec. 1949
	G. Georgel I, *E. T.* Oct. 1949
	G. Georgel II, *E. T.* Jan. 1949
PT. II, 1.	*V. I.* Oct. 1929
PT. II, 2.	*V. I.* Aug.–Sept. 1931
PT. III, 1.	*V. I.* Dec. 1931
PT. III, 2.	*V. I.* May 1933
PT. III, 3.	*V. I.* Aug.–Sept. 1933
PT. III, 4.	*Ignis* 1925
PT. III, 5.	*V. I.* Dec. 1930
REVIEWS	M. Bulard, *E. T.* July 1936
	C. Marston, *E. T.* Dec. 1936

PT. IV, 1.	*V. I.* April 1931
PT. IV, 2.	*V. I.* April 1932
PT. IV, 3.	*E. T.* Dec. 1936
REVIEWS	Enel I, *E. T.* Nov. 1936
	Enel II, *E. T.* Nov. 1937
	X. Guichard, *E. T.* June 1938
	N. Houssaye I, *E. T.* Jan. 1945
	N. Houssaye II, *E. T.* Jan. 1935
	Lettres d'Humanité, I and II:
	E. T. Jan.–Feb. 1948, Jan. 1945
	G. Dumézil, *E. T.* Dec. 1949

INDEX

Lightning Source UK Ltd.
Milton Keynes UK
20 September 2010

160100UK00003B/297/A